FAT DOG DON'T RUN NO RABBIT

PROMOTING CHANGE IN OVERPRIVILEGED CHILDREN AND THEIR FAMILIES

BY

FRANK L. QUINN, PhD

ISBN: 1-4140-3602-7 (e-book)
ISBN: 1-4140-3603-5 (Paperback)
ISBN: 1-4140-3604-3 (Dust Jacket)

Library of Congress Control Number: 2003098560

This book is printed on acid free paper.

Printed in the United States of America
Bloomington, IN

Cover illustration by Mary Lane Sloan

1stBooks - rev. 02/23/04

... the spirit of self-help is the root of all genuine growth in the individual; and exhibited in the lives of many, it constitutes the true source of national vigor and strength. Help from without is often enfeebling in its effects, but help from within invariably invigorates. Whatever is done for men or classes to a certain extent takes away the stimulus and necessity of doing it for themselves; and where men are subjected to over-guidance or over-government, the inevitable tendency is to render them comparatively helpless.

Samuel Smiles, *Self-Help,* **1859.**

CONTENTS

DEDICATION

This book is dedicated to the memory of my mother Dolly Dunn Quinn and to my father Frank L. Quinn, for helping me become an adult and letting go of my bicycle,

and

my wife Lane for helping me become a spouse and father,

and

my in-laws John and Mary Lane Pellett for giving me a wife,

and

my children, Mary Lane, Erin and Bryan for helping me become a parent,

and

all the Fat Dogs in the world, because no one is useless and even you can serve as a bad example.

PREFACE

In 1968 I was an undergraduate political science major at the University of North Carolina. A great deal of attention was being given to the study of the "underprivileged." In retrospect this seemed to be more the result of the massive guilt being felt by middle-class baby boomers as they ventured into an imperfect world, than the dawning of some truly *Aquarian Age.* Michael Harrington's book, *The Other America*, opened our eyes to the fate of the "have-nots" in our society and helped us understand how poverty often bred failure. After more than thirty years the debate still rages about how to remedy the ravages associated with being underprivileged. *Fat Dog Don't Run No Rabbit* is an attempt to explain why sometimes even the overprivileged fail to thrive.

The great accumulation of wealth and power by the United States during the twentieth century has made it the envy of the world, but it may also be what sows the seeds of future destruction. It is my contention that our largesse has led to the twin practices of overindulgence and overprotection, which in turn destroy the initiative of many young people in our society, through overprivilege. This cult of overprivilege not only disrupts the development of children into adults, but ultimately impedes the development of societies. The following discussion is an attempt to identify our contributions to this problem and to outline some strategies for overcoming them.

This is not a book of science, but is rather based upon my experience as a baby boomer, parent and twenty-five years as a therapist. This book is a collection of observations, reflections, folk wisdom and what was once called common sense. If you find this helpful please pass it on to someone else who might have a **Fat Dog.** If you do not find this book helpful please give it to your goat. After all, I could be wrong.

THINGS TO REMEMBER
AND
POINTS TO PONDER[*]

*YOU ARE MORE LIKELY YO ACT YOURSELF INTO
FEELING THAN TO FEEL YOUR WAY INTO ACTION*

ANYTHING WORTH DOING IS WORTH DOING POORLY

PEOPLE PUSH LIMITS IN ORDER TO FIND THEM

*THE RACE OFTEN GOES NOT TO THE SWIFT BUT TO
THOSE WHO JUST KEEP RUNNING*

IT IS BETTER TO TEACH THAN TO DO FOR

*THE QUICKEST WAY TO MAKE SOMEONE HATE YOU
IS TO OVERPROTECT THEM*

WE ARE WHAT WE ARE

YOU CAN LEAD A HORSE TO WATER... BUT A GOAT

WILL EAT ANYTHING

FAT DOG DON'T RUN NO RABBIT... HUNGRY DOG DO

---

[1]* *None of the above are original, just restatements of what we once knew but forgot.*

INTRODUCTION

Everyone knows a **Fat Dog.** In fact you may have several in your own family. **Fat Dogs** are the people who, like Peter Pan, never grow-up. Unfortunately, unlike Peter Pan, **Fat Dogs,** are not even good for fighting pirates. **Fat Dogs** seem destined to fail because they lack all motivation to succeed. Usually, **Fat Dogs** can be easily identified by anyone outside their immediate family, but their identity is almost always evident (even to their parents) during the launching phase of their development.

The true mark of a Fat Dog is the difficulty they encounter leaving home and becoming an adult.

Fat Dogs just don't seem to want to spread their wings and leave the nest, and when they do leave they seem to somehow bounce back. They may be attractive, intelligent and extremely gifted, but they seem to *never fulfill their potential.* Family members, teachers, coaches, friends and lovers often speak of how the **Fat Dog** *could have been somebody.*

For more than twenty years parents have been bringing their **Fat Dogs** to my office. Generally, these parents say that all they want is what most parents want ... to see their children *grow-up and be happy*. Most often I am not the first therapist that this family has sought out and sometimes I am not the last they will see. Many of these parents and their children, who come for help, learn how to not just survive but to flourish. Some don't survive.

A colleague, who read a draft of this book, said that I was too rough on parents and was not taking in to account all the complexities of modern life or the pressures on parents. My response to such statements is that I am "rough" on parents because I believe that raising children is the responsibility of parents and not as the popular saying goes "the village." This is not to say that parents are totally responsible for the behavior of their children, but rather parents are responsible for helping children learn to accept responsibility for their own behavior. As my mother was fond of saying,

"If you are smart enough to know how I screwed you up, you are smart enough to fix yourself."

Children do not grow-up in a vacuum and parents are always contributory in the development of a **Fat Dog.**

Regardless of poor parenting, bad genes, peer pressure, childhood trauma, stupid choices, social inequity or even acts of God, being an adult means accepting responsibility for your own behavior, making your own life and contributing to the greater good.

Fat Dogs are unable to become adults because their path has been impeded with privilege or obstructed by overprotection. The intent of this book is to help **Fat Dogs** break the chains of childhood and liberate their parents from providing eternal childcare.

THE FAT DOG FABLE

Once upon a time there was a kindly old man named Max. As a child Max had been very poor, but with hard work, sacrifice and perseverance he became quite prosperous. Although he had been too impoverished as a child to own something as frivolous as a pet, Max had hunted with and enjoyed the dogs of friends. He vowed that when he grew-up he would have a dog of his own and that he would love his dog more than anyone had ever loved a dog.

One day Max found a beautiful beagle puppy for sale. The Kennel Master said the puppy was from a long line of champion hunting dogs, and with the proper training he was sure the puppy would excel at rabbit hunting. Max took the puppy home and for a time they were both very happy.

The puppy became the center of Max's existence. Max fed the puppy from his own plate, let the puppy sleep with him and lavished the puppy with gifts and attention. Because he was very proud of the puppy's beauty and intelligence, Max took the puppy with him everywhere. Many people said that the puppy was just an extension of Max.

When people complained about the puppy's destructiveness or messiness, Max would just laugh and say, "But he is only a puppy." Max was always careful to clean up the mess or pay for any damage done by the puppy. When the puppy pleased Max, which was often, he was always rewarded with a tasty treat or a new toy. The puppy grew fat.

Because Max feared for his safety the puppy was never allowed to play with other animals or to stay outside alone. Often Max lectured the puppy on the dangers of the outside world, especially the forest. Max often attempted to discipline the puppy, but all it took was one pitiful whine by the puppy for Max's mind to flash to some dreadful "could-happen", and Max relented showering the puppy with tears and cookies.

When hunting season arrived both man and beagle were invited to a hunt. Max had dreamed of this moment many times. He knew that his "pride and joy" would show his bloodlines and lead the pack. His puppy would be the best rabbit-hunting dog ever. Max had dreamed of how he would puff up with pride, but smile modestly when the other hunters praised the puppy, because Max always knew the puppy was "special." The puppy just wanted to get outside and be with other dogs.

On the day of the hunt, the puppy (now rotund from too many treats and too little exercise) jumped for joy at the sight of so many dogs. Having never been with other dogs, the puppy did not know how to play or the rules of the pack. He soon grew tired and discouraged. The other dogs were irritated by his manners. He had no place in the pack.

When the pack set off to chase rabbits, the puppy hung close to his master whining and panting. Max gave the puppy a treat while apologizing to the other hunters. Later embarrassed in front of his friends by the puppy's incompetence and ill-temper, max shook his finger at the puppy. The puppy bit Max.

At this same hunt was a man named Nate, who like Max, had brought his puppy for the first time. Nate loved his puppy very much, but he understood that one day the puppy would be a dog. Nate had always encouraged the puppy to explore the world and to play with other dogs. Nate fed his puppy for sustenance and health not as a bribe or reward. He taught his puppy discipline, yet gave him freedom and love. The puppy grew to be a lean, strong, independent dog. When it was time for the puppy to hunt, Nate let him go...and the puppy went. **Fat Dog don't run no rabbit ... Hungry Dog do.**

CHAPTER ONE

WHAT IS A FAT DOG?

WHAT'S IN A NAME?

Most puppies and most children follow rather standard developmental tracks that lead to the acceptance of personal responsibility and the attainment of personal independence. When the process of this development is interrupted by overprivilege the result is often a **Fat Dog.** A **Fat Dog** is an individual or puppy who appears incapable of adulthood. These individuals are often described as:

- Lazy
- Fearful
- Unmotivated
- Easily frustrated
- Hedonistic
- Dependent
- Narcissistic
- Demanding
- Under-achieving
- Spoiled
- Cynical
- Grandiose

The first time I ever heard the term **Fat Dog** was when a colleague tried to explain to me why a particularly pampered patient had no motivation to change. After I listed the numerous strengths of this patient and the substantial support system at his disposal, I bemoaned his seemingly limitless ability to avoid adulthood. Dr. James Page, looked across the tennis net, smiled and simply said, "**Fat Dog** don't run no rabbit," (this old hunting adage reminds hunters not to pamper or overfeed their animals if they want them to be useful on a hunt). Since that day in 1977 I have observed and treated hundreds of **Fat Dogs**, and I have given much thought to reversing or preventing their condition.

PROFILE OF A FAT DOG

It is not politically correct these days to present pathological profiles because it is felt such profiles might be overgeneralized and lead to discrimination against groups. However, I think it might be useful to "profile" a **Fat Dog** in order to help with identification and treatment, so I have

3

listed some traits below which would be included in such a profile. These characteristics are representative of the **Fat Dogs** seen in my practice, but the sample might be too small to truly generalize from.

Age: Fat Dogs can be any age but the traits are most evident between ages 12 and 25. I have seen several patients who were 40+ that met the criteria for **Fat Dog** status.

Gender: In my practice males outnumber females at least 5 to 1. It should be noted that until recently there was significant societal pressure to maintain females in dependent roles and to some degree a female **Fat Dog** was not seen as pathological.

Race/ethnicity: Predominately white, but appears to cross racial boundaries. I would anticipate with the rise in the number of racial minorities among professionals there will be an increase in the number of minority **Fat Dogs**. Very few Asians todate have presented in my practice as **Fat Dogs**.

Religion: A friend suggested that all **Fat Dogs** were of the same religion…Me-ism.

Socioeconomic status: It would be logical that overprivilege would be an affliction of the rich or the upper-class (does anyone still use the term idle-rich leisure class), but the largest number of clients come from the newly rich or upper middle-class/professional groups. It should also be noted that I have had clients from the lower working class group, proving that income, education and social standing might be absolutes, but being overprivileged is relative.

Even though it might be easy to identify a **Fat Dog** in other families, it is often more difficulty to recognize the signs and symptoms in our own puppies. The checklist on the following page might prove helpful in establishing whether or not you are raising a **Fat Dog.** Don't turn the page if you are not ready for the truth.

<u>YOU MIGHT HAVE A FAT DOG IF...</u>

- Your child continually demonstrates a lack of courage
- Your child gives up easily
- Your child would rather cling to you than play with peers
- Your child is not liked by most children
- Your child's allowance is more than you save monthly
- Your child refuses to eat anything except "special" foods
- You believe your child's happiness is your responsibility
- You believe that your child can't make it in the "real world"
- You had rather tie your child's shoe than watch them struggle
- You choose to spend more time with your child than your spouse
- You have not taken a vacation in twenty-five years because you do not want your child to be alone
- You still layout your child's clothes after the child is older than six

- You blame your child's friends for those six D.U.I. arrests
- You worry that your child will suffer from "empty nest" syndrome when you and your spouse are dead
- Your thirty year old child lives at home, has no job, dresses better than you, only needs three more semesters to graduate and has a great tan

If you can answer yes to more than two of the above statements not only do you have a **Fat Dog**; you may need much more help than they do. **Fat Dogs** are not born that way, they are trained and become the way they are through a process or chronic overprivilege.

<u>OVERPRIVILEGE</u>

For the purpose of this discussion the term overprivileged will be used to encompass the concepts of overindulgence and overprotection. Although these terms are significantly different they can produce very similar outcomes, so I have chosen the more encompassing term, overprivilege, to describe both the process and the outcome that whelps **Fat Dogs.**

7

An individual might be considered overprivileged when the links between rights and responsibilities have been chronically and continuously evaded, eroded or ignored.

Parents and families contribute to the development of this pathogenic state by the mediation of consequences from behavior, which in turn deprives the **Fat Dog** of experience, motivation and respect.

OVERINDULGENCE

To indulge can be defined as "giving in to an inclination or desire." Certainly we indulge our loved ones and ourselves from time to time.

- We might indulge ourselves with a special dessert after a long day at the office.
- We may buy our five- year-old an ice cream for sitting still during a wedding.
- We might spend more on a special gift for our spouse than we had agreed to for purely sentimental reasons.

These are minor personal gifts that might mark the difference between flourishing and merely surviving in daily life. Unfortunately, when we indulge to excess (even with good things), we no longer flourish and indeed might not even survive.

The urge to indulge can be subtle and irresistible (*"What could it hurt, just this one time?"*). The urge to overindulge our children can seem almost natural (*"I don't care what the rules say, no child of mine will suffer like I did."*)

Another definition of indulgence, one that is particularly applicable to parenting, is "the granting of a special freedom or privilege," as in a papal or royal indulgence.

- A parent may indulge their teenager with an extension of a curfew on prom night.
- A child may be indulged with a vacation from chores during exam week.

These parental dispensations are usually one-time breeches in responsibilities or special allowances granted for special reasons. Such indulgences, when used sparingly, can be powerful rewards in shaping the behavior of a child. However, parents must become vigilant that these special indulgences do not become standard operating procedure. If parents are not vigilant the abuses once associated with papal indulgences and their effect on supplicants will be replicated in the behavior of the overindulged child.

Below you will find a brief list of how a child might be overindulged by well meaning parents:

- A child having an allowance with no expectation on how the money is to be spent/saved.
- An elementary school aged child having no set bedtime.
- A child in high school having no curfew.
- A child older than five having no regular chores.
- A child of any age having unrestricted use of computers, TV, play stations, CD players, etc.
- A child's desires outweighing the parents' or the family's in a decision effecting the family.
- Rudeness, disrespect or violence being excused without consequences.

<u>OVERPROTECTION</u>

Parents often feel caught between a desire to protect their children, thus insuring the survival of the species, and the knowledge that ultimately the child must learn to protect itself if the species is to survive. The image of a mother grizzly bear reared-up on her hind legs in defense of her cubs doesn't exaggerate the fury of a soccer-mom defending her young. In the wilderness this protective reaction lasts only a couple of years at most. In the suburbs it has been known to last for decades. Overprotection and hypervigilence on the part of parents can contribute to the failure to thrive as surely as neglect. The message that the overprotective parent sends to the child is *"the world is a dangerous place and <u>you</u> can not survive without <u>me</u>."*

Often parents ask, "How do I know if I'm being overprotective of my child?" My answer is usually,

"The primary goal of parenting is to help the child become an independent responsible adult. Actions that contribute to this goal are appropriate and actions that impede this goal are inappropriate."

11

This response sometimes just makes parents angry because they were hoping for a justification of rational pampering, rather than a reminder of the task at hand. There has to be a balance between setting limits for a child and encouraging the child to challenge the limits of their environment, but most imposed limits should be predicated on the developmental level of the child.

> **EXAMPLE: A toddler may be restricted from playing in a busy street to prevent premature death. An adolescent might be cautioned from playing in the street to prevent disaster. An adult is expected to navigate the same street with skill and caution.**

An adult who jaywalks may be run over just like a toddler who jaywalks, but the adult is infinitely more responsible. The difference is a matter of experience and maturity. If the toddler's parents perform their tasks of education and protection, and the toddler has the opportunity to learn and experience safe behavior, then as an adult the toddler will not require another person to hold their hand when they cross the street. If overprotected the toddler will always remain fearful, dependent and inadequate.

Below are some examples of how parents might overprotect their children:

- Shielding children from the "real" world.
- Choosing their children's friends.
- "Fixing" things for children.
- Being deaf to the phrase, "Me do it."
- Not allowing children to sleepover with friends.
- Not allowing children to handle sharp or "dangerous" objects.
- Intervening between their child and authority figures.

A final consideration, in determining whether or not one is being overprotective, is history.

Is there a pattern of protection, mediation and or parental involvement that prohibits limited-trial learning by the child?

If the answer is **YES**, and the practice continues well beyond what is considered reasonable, the parent is overprotective.

If however, the protective act is isolated in nature or required by clear and present overwhelming danger, the parent is only being prudent.

If the act is deemed overprotective, we might wonder whom the parent is protecting, the child or themselves.

CHAPTER TWO

THE FREEDOM TO FAIL,
FAT DOG(MA) AND FREE WILL

FAT DOG(MA) AND FREE WILL

Theologians and philosophers have debated the concept of free will for centuries and it is likely that they will debate its importance for centuries to come. My expertise is in neither theology nor philosophy, but it seems to me that free will must fulfill a psychological need of humans to feel in control and self-directed. The constant unwavering love of a parent, like the love of God, does not insure that the child feels lovable or worthy of being loved. Feeling lovable is ultimately predicated on self-worth. Self-worth is predicated on a sense that one is in control of their destiny and has some choice in their behavior.

The true value of free will is that it provides a process for the development of value.

- To the theologian free will allows for the process of redemption and the acceptance of grace through sin.
- To the philosopher free will allows for the process of learning through experience.

- To the parent free will allows for the child to develop into an adult.

Certainly being protected and sheltered from harm communicates that one is loved, but when taken to the extreme of overprotection, it erodes self-worth, inhibits the development of self-reliance and communicates despair. There is a reason that Adam and Eve must leave the Garden other than punishment for eating the apple. They must leave the Garden to become adults.

In the early stages of childhood the parent must make choices and decisions for the survival of the infant. As the child grows to adulthood it must experience the fullness and limits of free will.

Responsibility logically flows from choice. If a child is not free to choose, then they are less likely to accept personal responsibility and to blame others. But, if a child is free to choose without consequences they become less responsible and more dependent.

Fat Dogs never experience the fullness of free will, because they are either offered too few choices or too many choices, and they rarely suffer the consequences of their choices.

Whether by parents or by God, the greatest love is demonstrated by letting-go of our children and recognizing the importance of the process engendered by choice. In life, as in theology, only when an individual possesses free will do they truly possess the ability to flourish. For a child to develop into an adult, and not become a **Fat Dog,** parents must be prepared to let-go while remembering that free will always allows for the freedom to fail.

THE FREEDOM TO FAIL

The freedom to fail is necessary if an individual is to succeed and to internalize the lessons of their own success or failure. Anyone who succeeds solely with the help of others or who is overprotected by others finds it hard to gain in self-worth or self-confidence from such an exercise. Indeed it usually has the reverse effect making them feel *less.*

(i.e. use*less*, help*less*, worth*less*)

When denied the freedom to fail individuals may initially become vain, narcissistic and grandiose, but with time they lapse into a debilitating state of self-doubt and pessimism. Without failure or at least the freedom to fail, individuals often lack the lessons of humility or humanity that teach them how to balance rights and responsibilities.

Small failures early in life allow an individual to problem-solve with few lasting negative consequences. If these failures are accompanied by a few small successes the individual also learns *hopefulness*. It is important to note that dealing with failure presents children with the opportunity to practice overcoming frustration.

Successfully dealing with frustration is essential in the enjoyment of life, the development of optimism, the accomplishment of independence and the attainment of personal happiness.

The *fear of failure*, by both the parent and the unweaned **Fat Dog**, is often exhibited through an inordinate amount of perfection and rigidity. A sign of this is when parents are heard saying, "Anything worth doing is worth doing right." Consequently, the well-trained **Fat Dog** responds by doing very little and assuming that whatever he does do will not be quite right. This passive-pessimistic attitude results in one form of *learned helplessness.* It would be infinitely better for the parents to say something like, **"Anything worth doing is worth doing poorly."** This type of statement would encourage children to take the necessary risks inherent in learning and to accept the fact that they may have many temporary failures. Parents need to communicate and model that the strength of one's ego is not a function of perfectionism, but a willingness to face the challenges of life.

THE PARABLE OF THE BICYCLE

Once there was a man who wanted to teach his daughter to ride a bicycle. The man remembered his own joyful childhood, when bike riding was his greatest pleasure, and he wanted to share the fun with his daughter. Unfortunately, he also remembered the falls, the accidents, near accidents and bruises that often accompany riding a bicycle. He could not imagine letting his beautiful precious daughter suffer the way he had. He armored his daughter in heavy gloves, kneepads, a helmet and safety glasses. Only then did he grab the bike seat his daughter was mounted on and begin to push. The young girl screamed and pedaled. When the man finally let go, the girl pedaled a few wobbly feet, slowed, lurched to the left and fell toward the cruel concrete. Like a flash the adrenaline propelled father dashed forward and grabbed the young girl just inches from disaster. The young girl burst into tears of fright and clutched at her father's neck. The man checked her for injuries and assured her that he would never let her fall. Then, they started the process over, with the father trotting behind the bicycle holding the seat, while

21

begging the girl to go slower and be more careful. They both eventually tired, but were thankful that no real harm had been done. When the father expressed his fears to the little girl she too became terrified of falling and begged him to never let go of the bicycle again. He promised that he would not. Today you can sometimes still see them in the park. A middle-aged woman frantically pedaling a sixteen inch bicycle, while a gray-haired old gentleman trots behind her holding on to the bike seat. He has never let go and she has never fallen.

Fat Dogs are phobic of failure, having been trained to be so by well-meaning parents, who do not understand the process of failure just the state of failure.

In order to protect themselves from the trauma of failure **Fat Dogs** develop numerous psychological defenses. Unfortunately, these defenses actually prevent success because they disrupt the learning process. These defenses are much like the father who protected his daughter from failure and pain by preventing her from learning to ride a bicycle. Some of the most common defenses employed by **Fat Dogs** are listed below:

FAT DOG DEFENSE MECHANISMS

APATHY

Fat Dogs have limited interests. They appear to care about very little except their own comfort. They may appear completely indifferent to the conditions of others.

AMOTIVATION

Fat Dogs appear to exhibit little internal drive and may be almost completely immune to the blandishments or bribes of others. Remember, all the natural needs of the Fat Dog have already been oversupplied. Why chase rabbits if someone feeds you lobster every night?

CYNICISM

Fat Dogs openly question the altruism of others, exhibiting none themselves, and constantly saying "What is in this for me?"

GRANDIOSITY

Fat Dogs often affect an air of superiority far beyond what they deserve. They exaggerate their own importance and assume that their wish is everyone else's command. Unfortunately, people often reinforce this belief system. I have never met a parent of a Fat Dog who did not think their child was "above average."

ANESTHESIA

Fat Dogs soothe their pain/fear through short-term gratification. They are prone to abuse food, sex, drugs, etc. They do not wish to feel uncomfortable and will avoid it at all costs.

PRE-EMPTIVE FAILURE

Fat Dogs are masters at contriving failures, which trigger the protective systems of their parents. They are so fearful of failure they are continually willing to appear incompetent.

LOWERED EXPECTATIONS

Fat Dogs are known for their grandiosity, but they habitually settle for less than their own best effort. They are unwilling to pay the price of success, whether it is practice, study, work, etc. Therefore, they lower their goals and cut their costs. They might whine about their situation, but they do as little to change it as possible.

PROJECTION

Fat Dogs actually feel "less than" and they assume everyone else *is the way they feel.* In short, they project that everyone is bad, weak, scared, incompetent, narcissistic, lonely and stupid.

BLAME

Fat Dogs believe that there is always enough blame to go around, as long as they do not have to accept any themselves. It is always someone or something else's fault according to the Fat Dog or their parents.

The **Fat Dog** may exhibit all of the above defenses at different times, but it is doubtful that any **Fat Dog** would exhibit all of them all of the time. When the defenses become so embedded that they become the foundation of the **Fat Dog's** personality, they contribute to the development of a personality disorder hereafter known as **CYNO-REGRESSIVE PERSONALITY DISORDER (CRPD)** or as it is more commonly known **PERMANENT PUPPYHOOD.**

Regardless of how well they are defended every **Fat Dog** will ultimately fail, due to their fear of failure and the intercession of their parents.

CHAPTER THREE

A PACK OF PUPPIES

"The thing that impresses me most about America is the way parents obey their children"
(King Edward VIII)

<u>PERMANENT PUPPIES</u>

During the quarter of a century that I have been a therapist many **Fat Dogs** and their parents have come to me for help. Usually they come to my office after some crisis has made it impossible to ignore the child's failure to thrive. The crisis might be academic, financial, emotional, legal or a combination of all of these, but the bottomline is that the child is not making the transition into adulthood. The child and the parents appear stuck developmentally, with no clear plan for productive change.

In this chapter I have attempted to describe cases which are representative of the **Fat Dog** phenomenon. Please note that while these cases are true, they are not real. The cases are true in that they did happen. The cases are not real because they are compilations of characters and experiences, but do not represent any one person or case.

PUPPY # 1: ADAM

At twenty-nine Adam was still referred to as the "baby" in his affluent family of high-achievers. Although there were six children in this blended family, everyone agreed that Adam was the most intelligent and had the most potential. He had the looks of a tired and troubled Jimmy Buffet wannabe. He pondered each question as though seeking for some deep truth or "right answer." Often he would smile and say, "I know what you are getting at," even to standard interview questions like, "where did you grow-up?" Although Adam had been in and out of college for over ten years and had majored in a dozen subjects, he had never completed a degree. He was currently living in a storefront owned by his family. He drank and smoked pot abusively. Adam had a few friends and even an occasional girlfriend, but most often found himself alone once the veneer of his charm wore thin. Adam was "supporting himself" at this time with odd jobs and the kindness of friends or family. He seemed to always be hatching some new "get-rich-quick scheme" and was always boasting of how independent he was. Of course he did have a free *place to live, the use of a family-company owned vehicle, a six-figure trust fund and an allowance from his father of $100 per week. Adam's mother died shortly after his birth and his father saw him as a "failed seed." Adam was rigid, easily frustrated and liked to intellectualize. He wanted everyone to believe that nothing bothered him, but he saw himself as a failure and so did his family. The family had become so embarrassed by Adam that they began to exclude him from family functions. The precipitating event that brought Adam to therapy was a Thanksgiving dinner fiasco. When asked to remove his hat at the table, Adam became argumentative and in the midst of the ensuing screaming match he "accidentally" stomped an aged aunt's poodle.*

After two years of therapy Adam demonstrated marked progress. He had a full-time job that was not a gift from a relative. He was back in school and making excellent grades. He had established a long-term relationship with a young professional woman and was contemplating marriage. His relationship with his family had become more distant, but also more respectful. Adam's father even acknowledged that "that boy is acting like a man."

Unfortunately, at this point Adam's grandfather died leaving him more money than he could ever spend. The last I heard of Adam was that he had moved to South America and had begun an independent pharmaceutical business.

PUPPY # 2: MYRON

Myron was a very bright adolescent with sensitive features and an impish grin. He came from a family that appeared loving,_prosperous and intact. Myron's father was a respected_attorney who had made a reputation, and a fortune, at an early age representing consumers. Myron's mother was professor in the school of Social Work at a local college. Although, Myron was described as a "willful child", he had caused little trouble in his family until he dropped out of school midway through his senior year. Shortly after dropping out of school Myron moved in with some friend, started sporting numerous body piercings and tattoos, and began experimenting with various drugs. The shocked parents tried threats, force and bribery to get Myron to return home. At this point the parents announced that they were cutting Myron off. They reported that Myron *was begging on the streets and had been reduced to eating a dead cat that he had found. The parents could not figure out what had gone wrong and began to blame everyone from Myron's friends to his teachers. At one point it was even suggested that the root of Myron's problem was not making the little league team when he was eleven. It was at about this time that I discovered that the parent's idea of cutting Myron off meant providing him with an apartment, a car and $1000/month. The parents could not understand why Myron did not wish to come home, get a job or demonstrate any outward signs of stumbling toward adulthood.*

When the parents were convinced to really cut him off, Myron bottomed-out in a very short period of time and asked to come in from the cold. Myron continued to test his parents for some time, but by consistently allowing him to face the consequences of his own actions and expecting respect, they were able to help Myron re-launch himself. Today Myron owns a small health food store, has a wife and two children and is active in local politics. Although he exhibits few scars from his life on the streets, it is rumored that somewhere on his body he rather indiscreetly bears the tattoo … UNREPENTANT.

<u>PUPPY #3: PAUL</u>

Paul had been asked to leave four separate colleges by his twentieth birthday. He was well-groomed, dressed in expensive clothes and driving a $90,000 sports car. Paul had never had a real job, but also seemed to never have less than $500 in his pocket. He was living at home with his parents and paternal grandmother. His father was a judge and local political boss. Paul's mother, a former homecoming queen at a state college, was very active in civic organizations and was known as "the queen of charity." The grandmother refused to be seen in public without a hat and gloves, and as she was fond of saying, "could trace her roots to every good family in the state." The family owned large tracts of land and made most of their money from cotton and tobacco. During the previous four years Paul had acquired over a dozen speeding tickets (most of which seemed to disappear), wrecked three cars, bounced numerous checks (even when he had plenty of *cash), and actually stabbed one of the few young women willing to date him more than once. Paul had a penchant for lying and grandiosity (he boasted of serving tennis balls at 200 mph), and developed the bad habit of threatening anyone who disagreed with him. His family continued to bail him out of trouble even after numerous therapists said that this was contributing to the problem. Although the parents ranted, raved, screamed, cried, cursed, threatened, bribed and cajoled they never followed through with any punishment very long. The parents said they only wanted to know two things when they brought Paul to see me. First they wanted to know what it would take to make Paul happy. Second they wanted to know why Paul hated them. They did not like my answers or suggestions for change so they pulled Paul out of therapy with me and found another therapist.*

Two months short of his twenty-third birthday Paul called his current therapist and said, "I want to thank you for all the help you have given me, but I have decided to kill myself." He then hung-up the phone, laid down on his mother's side of the bed, took his father's favorite pistol and shot himself. He left a note saying, "I hope I have not ruined your plans." It was the night of his parent's twenty-fifth wedding anniversary.

PUPPY # 4: ANGEL

Intelligent, quick-witted, physically mature beyond her thirteen years, and in complete control, Angel listened, with no hint of remorse, while her parents recounted her many misdeeds. Her parents brought her in for therapy because they found out she was sexually active. It had not been until they walked in on her having sex with a young man six years her senior, that they realized it might not be a good idea to allow guests in her bedroom. When her mother walked in that fateful afternoon on the "tutoring session", Angel yelled at her for not respecting her privacy rights. The mother continually apologized for not knocking through out the first appointment. The father, an ex-Navy fighter pilot and currently a successful dentist, said nothing during the session, but tearfully asked for his daughter's forgiveness as they shuffled out of my door. They did not return for three years. By age sixteen, Angel had been admitted to psychiatric hospitals on six occasions, diagnosed with an eating disorder and a substance abuse disorder, had three abortions, wrecked a car (paralyzing a friend), run away from home too many times to count, contracted gonorrhea, and had scored 1476 on her SAT. She quit going to school her junior year because she had accrued twenty-six unexcused absences before Christmas. When her father offered to send her to Europe to find herself and to get away from her bad friends, Angel offered to housesit while her parents went to Europe instead. Returning from Europe, the parents were literally met at the airport by angry neighbors complaining about the non-stop party Angel had while her parents were abroad.

Angel is now married to an accountant and has a son. Angel is a psychology graduate student. Her life began to turn around shortly after her mother asked if Angel should be allowed to go on her senior cruise. I told the mother that as Angel had just been released from yet another hospital, where her parents placed her for "drinking and screwing", that it did not make sense to lock her on a floating hotel for a week with 1,200 teenagers who were all intent on "drinking and screwing" as much as possible. For some reason this comment sunk in and Angel's parents began to say ...NO! It took several years before Angel began to resemble an adult, but few people who know her today would be able to guess about her adolescence.

<u>PUPPY # 5: BEAU</u>

Beau's mother cleaned our office in the evenings. During the day she *worked full-time as a nursing tech at a local hospital. Her total income on which she supported a family of four, was just over $16,000/ year. The first time I saw Beau he was wearing a pair of $150 basketball shoes, heavy gold chains, a Ralph Lauren shirt and Calvin Klein jeans. Beau was six feet tall, weighed over two hundred pounds and had just turned twelve. This man-child could have easily passed for much older had he not constantly whined and acted like a much younger child. The family, consisting of Beau, the mother, two younger siblings and a disabled grandmother, all shared a three-bedroom apartment in a government housing project. Beau had his own bedroom. He liked to eat and he liked new clothes. Beau did not like work, school, chores or anyone who told him what to do. Beau was seen in my office after he got in* *trouble taking lunch money from smaller children and threatening a teacher. His mother complained that the charges were trumped-up and that it was a "racial thing." Beau never came back after the first session even though I offered to see him pro bono, because he didn't feel like answering anymore questions.*

Several months after seeing me, Beau broke his mother's nose when she tried to get him up in time for church. She missed work for the first time in over a decade, because this injury required surgery. Still, she protected and defended her "baby." Often she would tell anyone who would listen that her baby would be a big sports star one-day if people would quit picking on him. Before he graduated from high school Beau attracted the attention of colleges all over the country, which recruited him to play football. Shortly before graduation another teenager who claimed Beau had raped his sister shot Beau. Beau survived the shooting but the wound ended his athletic career. Today he is still his mother's "baby". A six foot seven inch, three hundred and eighty-two pound baby.

PUPPY # 6: TIFFANY

Tif, as her parents called her, was an eight-year-old spoiled brat when she strode into my office like a queen visiting the peasants. It was clear that Tif was very smart and quite well educated (she had been a voracious independent reader since four). Both of her parents were fast-track banking executives and this only child had not been born until both parents were past forty. Tif had twenty-three pairs of assorted sneakers in a rainbow of colors to match all her outfits. She was generally too well mannered and proper around adults, although she could fly into a rage if she did not get her way or the attention she felt entitled to. Although her grades were excellent all he teachers were glad to see her move on to the next grade. Children found Tif bossy, prissy, self-centered, overly competitive, mean spirited, no fun and in general obnoxious. She had no friends, no playmates (unless her parents arranged "social interaction time" with the children of people who worked for them) and more toys than FAO Schwartz. Tif always had to win, and she would lie or cheat to do so. She never met a rule that applied to her. If by some chance she was not first or lost in a competition, she flew into a rage or whined, pouted and cried. Her parents brought Tif to see me because they feared she was being picked on by other children and that this would erode her self-confidence. Tif did not let her mother complete one sentence during the interview without interruption. The mother, looking deeply distressed, accepted this behavior without comment and kept feeding Tif from a seemingly endless supply of candy in her purse. The parents wanted my blessing to move Tif to another school where the "other children would not be so rude" to their princess. When I told them that so far they had been extremely fortunate that another child had not beaten Tif to a pulp, they almost left my office. When I told them it was taking all my control as an adult and the fear of losing my license to keep me from intervening physically, the mother did leave in a great indignant huff. The father admitted that often he wanted to "tan her little hide." I assured him that I did not think that would be necessary, but that I saw no hope of Tiffany improving unless both parents were willing to set more appropriate behavioral limits for the child. In fact since the parents were the only two people willing to tolerate Tif's behavior I predicted that her social circle would eventually consists only of them.

Four years later the princess was back in my office. She had assaulted her 94-year-old great-grandmother, because the old lady had the audacity to beat Tif at Scrabble. Unfortunately, the parents were still unwilling to be parents; they wanted to be her "best friend." Today, T.S. (as she calls herself) has stumbled into the adult world, but not adulthood. Her academic record, competitiveness and ruthless lack of compassion made her a natural to succeed in the legal profession. Tif still lives with her parents, continually has money problems (despite a high six-figure income), is hated/feared by her colleagues, weighs more than most offensive linemen in the NFL and has never had a meaningful intimate relationship.

PUPPY # 7 & # 8: TYLER & TORI

Tyler (17) and Tori (16) were the teenage son and daughter of a dot.com baby millionaire. Their father made a fortune well before his thirtieth birthday or his first relationship with a woman. Their mother had become their father's secretary the day after she graduated from high school. When he turned forty-five the father decided to sell everything, leave California, spend time with the family and find himself. After settling the family into a renovated antebellum mansion on the battery in Charleston the father became seriously committed to making up for the perceived disadvantages of his childhood and the lack of time he spent with his children when they were younger and he was working 80 hrs/week. The mother was completely overwhelmed by a social order predicated on ancestors who predated the American Revolution by at least three generations. Tyler and Tori had developed attitudinal problems before leaving the Silicon Valley, but they became impossible to live with once they realized the move to South Carolina was permanent. Tyler would not leave the house for days and devoted most of his time to playing fantasy games on the Internet with his cyber friends. When he did deign to interact with the family his darkly shrouded wraithlike figure was in the room only a few smoldering minutes before a yelling match would erupt. Tori would leave the mansion, mostly at night and without telling anyone, to conduct her own experiments in racial and *socio-economic diversity. She refused to go to school, because as she pointed out to her parents, there was no way she could ever spend all the money she already had in her trust fund ($3,000,000) and the educational system was nothing more than a flunky for capitalist pigs. By this time both parents were drinking too much and the mother was having an affair with her tennis instructor. The father would have most likely been having an affair also but he was having difficulty with impotency.*

The parents came asking what could be done to help their children. By focusing on their marriage and redefining their parenting goals they were able to effect remarkable change in a rather brief time frame. Tyler was emancipated. Tori was placed with a Mennonite family on a dairy farm for two months. The parents began acting like adults. Within 90 days this family had restored some semblance of self-respect and direction to itself. Tyler is now a sophomore engineering student at Georgia Tech and Tori is a freshman at Duke. The parents have left the battery, bought a farm in Jasper County and devote much of their time and fortune to improving literacy in rural low-country South Carolina.

PUPPY # 9: JOHN

John was really named Juan, but he was embarrassed by his Latino heritage so he only answered to John. His grandparents came from Mexico to pick tomatoes forty years ago. They had less than nothing, but worked very hard. John's father went to Clemson on a soccer scholarship and became a very successful manager at a large textile mill. The resources of two generations in this family were poured on John like water. He was sent to private schools, expensive camps, piano lessons, tennis/golf lessons, riding lessons and shooting lessons. John was handsome, dashing, athletic, charming and lazy. So many things came easy to him; he never learned to try anything difficult. Women were so attracted to John that by the time he was a senior in high school he was being courted by women in their thirties and forties, some of whom had husbands and all of whom had money. John came to my office because he was involved with the young trophy wife of a prominent businessman and had assaulted the man when he was discovered. John's attorney had suggested an evaluation.

John did not want help; he just didn't want to go to jail. Eventually the charges were dropped and John left town. For the last several years he has lived with a variety of women as their "guest." John has never had a job, yet he continues to wear expensive clothes, drive fancy cars and spend lots of other people's money. He still looks great.

Perhaps you have recognized one of these puppies, perhaps not. Please remember **Fat Dogs** are not born they are made, any child can become one if trained to be so.

CHAPTER FOUR

IS MY DOG FAT?

OR

HOW TO RECOGNIZE OVERPRIVILIGED CHILDREN AND THEIR FAMILIES

Many people have asked me to provide a way to assess the potential for overprivilige and the development of a **Fat Dog** in their family. Because human behavior is influenced by its context it is important to examine the behavior of the family system and not just the potential **Fat Dog.** The following are general observations made over the years about **Fat Dogs and their families** (many of these observations are common in most dysfunctional families, especially if substance abuse is involved):

- **THERE IS ALWAYS A VICTIM**
- **THERE IS ALWAYS AT LEAST ONE MARTYR**
- **THERE IS ALWAYS A GOOD REASON FOR THE EXCEPTIONS TO BEHAVIORAL LIMITS GRANTED THE FAT DOG... THE FAT DOG IS SPECIAL**
- **THERE IS ALWAYS WASTEFULNESS AND AVARICE**
- **THERE IS ALWAYS CYNICISM**
- **THE STATED GOAL OF THE PARENTS IS THE HAPPINESS OF THE CHILD**
- **FAT DOGS DON'T PLAY**

- **THE FAMILY COMMUNICATES INDIRECTLY**
- **PARENTAL RELATIONSHIPS ARE UNDERDEVELOPED**
- **THE FAT DOG HATES AND SHOWS DISRESPECT FOR THE PARENTS, AND THE PARENTS FEEL OVERWHELMED AND BETRAYED**
- **THE FAT DOG DISPLAYS SOCIAL DISINTEREST**

If after perusing the above list you have the uneasy feeling that your system, or the family of someone you know, might be in the process of developing a **Fat Dog**, the information in this chapter can help you clarify this.

THERE IS ALWAYS A VICTIM

The victim is almost always the **Fat Dog** and is also the identified patient when the family seeks professional help. This may be somewhat obscured by the fact that the victim is often treated as a prince or princess by the over-indulgent family. The family needs the victim to maintain the precarious state of equilibrium it is seeking. The family may even derive its identity from the victim, e.g. "parents of a runaway", "brother of a dopehead", or "co-dependent." In short the specialness of the victim adds purpose and meaning to the life of the family. Yet, even if the family treats the victim as royalty, the specialness of this position implies some form of inadequacy.

The Fat Dog may naturally possess certain inadequacies, but the actions of the over-indulgent family magnify, ritualize and in some cases glorify these shortcomings.

Many therapists believe that the identified victim (patient) is the healthiest member of the family, but it is the symptoms exhibited by the victim that often bring the family to treatment.

There is a very old joke about a family that brings its eldest son to see a therapist because the boy thinks he is a chicken. The weary therapist interrupts the family's long list of complaints and says, "I understand, I understand. You want me to convince the boy that he is not a chicken." The mother promptly speaks up and says, "Oh no Doctor, we want you to teach him not to defecate in the kitchen, but we still need the eggs."

Thus, even though the victim must ultimately assume responsibility for their own behavior, their maladaptive behavior is often shaped and reinforced by a well-meaning but needy family... who still "need the eggs."

Continued indulgence and protection develops a deep sense of inadequacy within the victim. This feeling becomes more exaggerated by the enabling of the family, until the victim not only accepts the role, but with much frustration and anger begins to realize that they are being victimized. The behavior associated with being a victim may vary over developmental stages, making it difficult to identify the victim as a **Fat Dog.** Below is a list of behaviors that might help identify the victim as a **Fat Dog** at different developmental stages:

Toddler to pre-school: Stubbornness, fearfulness, whining, rudeness, crying, fussiness about food-clothing-etc., unwillingness to go to bed, tantrums, clinginess, helplessness, inordinate anger, over-attachment.

School-age to pre-teen: Aggressiveness, violence, dishonesty, cruelty, fear of failure or losing, overwhelming need for attention, manipulative humor, pessimism, fighting, lack of confidence, difficulty maintaining friendships, limit pushing.

Adolescence: Apathy, affected superiority, indifference, ego-centricism, mood-swings, inappropriate risk-taking, underachievement, inappropriate dependence on parents, lack of motivation, difficulty with authority, blaming others. **It should be noted that many parents**

maintain it is impossible to distinguish between normal adolescence and any aberrant state.

Young adulthood: Inability to attain or maintain employment, chronic underemployment, grandiosity, hedonism, extravagance, lack of goals, unhealthy relationships, amotivation, excessive use of mood-altering substances, open hostility toward parents, minor legal problems, continued dependence on parents, easily frustrated, lack of perseverance, exaggerated sense of self-worth, anxiety.

Adulthood: This state is impossible achieve for a **Fat Dog** or a victim. What is observable is an extended version of adolescence with the consequences of their behavior becoming increasingly more devastating to *others*. Throughout this period the **Fat Dog** whines about how difficult it is to be an adult to anyone who will listen.

THERE IS ALWAYS A MARTYR

Every over-indulgent family has at least one martyr. The martyr is usually the opposite-sexed parent of the victim, but sometimes siblings and even grandparents bear this cross. It is the energy and the dynamics between the martyr and the **Fat Dog** that define the parameters of the family's pathology. It is their "dance" which both frightens and enchants outsiders, because outsiders are never sure who is "leading."

The martyr is easy to spot. Willing to sacrifice the literal coat off their back, the martyr will stand in a driving rain or blizzard unprotected if this sacrifice will spare the health or hairdo of the Fat Dog. Like the portrait of Dorian Gray withering in the attic, the visage of the martyr often reflects the intercepted worldly consequences of the Fat Dog's behavior.

Martyrs might complain, cajole, demand, whine, threaten, sigh and even whimper. They are often heard saying things like:

"Okay, but this is the last time!"

or

"I just want you to be happy."

However, it is the terrible silence of the martyr that is the most destructive.

The times that the martyr chooses not to speak, or bites their tongue, or sugar coats reality, these are the times that the martyr passively obstructs the passage of their children from egocentric "puppies" to worthwhile adults.

Martyrs often protest that they are only motivated by love. They justify the mediation of consequences with the sweep of their hand and seem to really believe that they are "helping" the **Fat Dog** when they over-indulge or over-protect them.

The real motivation in the behavior of martyrs is personal fear or avoidance of personal pain.

The martyr is unwilling to face many of life's most challenging yet rewarding tasks, such as helping children become adults, because they are afraid. The martyr looks at a twenty-year-old moving into their own apartment, but they still see a six-year-old on the first day of school.

The martyr needs the Fat Dog so much that it is impossible for the martyr to believe that the Fat Dog does not need them just as much.

The martyr believes that the **Fat Dog** will always need them, and they insure this by indulging their own fears.

In the event of real danger the martyr would gladly change places with the **Fat Dog,** because their chronic intervention has trained them to believe that the **Fat Dog** would perish if left to fend for themselves. How this thought process might work, even in healthy families, was demonstrated to me several years ago by own father.

During a late night reflective conversation, my father shared that he was terrified by the prospect of me being drafted during the Vietnam War. He said that he often daydreamed about volunteering to re-enlist if the Selective Service Board would not draft me. My father reasoned that though he was in his mid forties and out of service for more than two decades, he could survive the war and I would not. I won't argue that his experience as an island-hopping Marine in World War II would have given him an advantage, but at eighteen I was an Eagle Scout, an athlete and had spent most of my life in the woods and swamps of eastern North Carolina. It is possible I would have perished in Vietnam if drafted, or it is possible that I would have possessed the skills and luck to survive that my father had a quarter of a century before. The point is that his willingness to sacrifice himself rather than face the pain of my death or even its potential demonstrates the way martyrs rationalize their behavior.

The difference between the martyr and the reaction of a healthy parent is that the healthy parent may possess the same fears as the martyr, but the healthy

parent does not allow these fears to interfere with responsible and respectful actions.

My father may have anguished over my fate in the jungles of Southeast Asia, and he may not have been in favor of the Vietnam War, but if I had been drafted he would have done what was done by his mother. He would have let me go. My father loved me enough to let me be, regardless of his own pain or fear. There is no greater love than this, even being willing to die in the place of another does not match this type of love. As a child it always bothered me that God let his son Jesus die on the cross. From the perspective of adulthood and a parent of many years I now understand that story in a different light. Jesus was allowed to fulfill his destiny on the cross, by a father who was with him, but was too respectful to protect him.

THERE IS ALWAYS A "GOOD REASON" FOR THE EXCEPTIONS

When confronted with the narcissistic demands of a Fat Dog, the parents often proffer "good reasons" why this behavior is not only tolerated

but also reinforced and encouraged by them. These justifications are usually supported by an emotional logic that is in direct conflict with the parents' stated parenting goal

<u>**Fat Dog's**</u> <u>demand:</u> "I need more gas money for my Z-3."

<u>Parents' logic:</u> We want him to have the fun that we didn't. He can't work and go to school. He looks great in that car. We want him to like us better than we liked our parents. We must give him what he wants.

<u>Parents' stated goal:</u> We want to raise an independent responsible adult.

If this breach in logic occurs only rarely it can be forgiven as an example that parents are human. If the emotional logic regularly replaces the stated parental goal, then the stage of this family drama is set for tragedy, not comedy.

Parents (and grandparents) of the Great Depression present another example of this emotional logic override when they say things like, "I had to walk three miles to school in the snow and no child of mine is going to be without a car." Certainly no parent would wish suffering on their child and human progress is predicated on each generation trying to improve the life of the next generation, but it is difficult to understand how endowing a sixteen year old with a thirty thousand dollar SUV is less harmful than allowing them to walk to school. What these parents of the Great Depression forget is that it was their own struggles with privation that made them independent and responsible. To rob children of the opportunity to struggle is no less consequential than to deprive them of attending school. In fact many of the Great Depression parents extol the value of the "school of hard knocks."

All children are special to their parents, but **Fat Dogs** are treated more special by their parents. These parents are quick to latch on to the perceived specialness of their children while denying the commonality that they share with all children. This phenomenon was unabashedly demonstrated on a TV show called "thirtysomething" several years ago. In several episodes of this show the central characters wallowed in self-centered pathos suggesting that they were the only humans to ever have offsprings.　　This frenzy did not diminish but rather escalated to the point that it was evident these uber-parents thought the fate of all mankind rested entirely on the selection of a pre-school for their unborn wunderkind.　If there is a sequel called "fiftysomething" using the same characters, I am sure there will be at least one **Fat Dog.**

Certainly there are children who warrant special treatment and may be at some risk of becoming **Fat Dogs**. Who can blame the parents of a child with cerebral palsy for being afraid if their child is not given special treatment in a swimming pool.　Who can not empathize with the parents of a child with cystic fibrosis who are afraid to let their child spend the night with a friend.　Certainly these are legitimate fears and legitimate reasons for special treatment, but they can also be traps if the parents do not allow their children the risks of life.

For over a decade my wife directed a camp for children with special needs (in less politically correct times it was referred to as a crippled children's camp) and it was my privilege to observe parents summon the courage to allow their special children the opportunity to become just children.　It is difficult to measure the fear these parents must have felt when they left their special children in the care of strangers at this camp built in a pine swamp on an alligator infested lake. It is also difficult to fathom the amount of pride and joy, shared by both parent and child, nine days later when the child could point to their awards for archery, swimming or some other activity *just like other children*. Often this was the first realization that these parents had that there was no "good reason" to treat their child as "special." Parents who can accept this will not further handicap their children by teaching them to be **Fat Dogs.**

Perhaps one of the most often cited "good reasons" parents present as an excuse for special treatment is low self-esteem. Many parents say they do not wish to damage the fragile self-esteem of their child, so the do not deal with the child in a respectful and honest manner.

These parents are loathe to give constructive criticism, set reasonable boundaries, expect respect or just say no, because they think this might cause their child too much frustration or internal conflict. These parents do not seem to

understand that self-esteem is something that can only be developed, enhanced and maintained through ordeal. Frustration, sacrifice, perseverance and introspection form the crucible from which self-esteem emerges.

A local guidance counselor related the following story to me and I think it illustrates what can happen when parents get confused about the development of self-esteem.

Mr. and Mrs. Jones came to see me about their son Tom, who was in academic trouble and in peril of losing his athletic eligibility. Tom was a surly nineteen-year-old junior with a D- average and no evident interest other than football. The parents said, "Tom eats and sleeps football, and if he has to give it up we don't think he could go on living." Both parents worked very hard so their children could have things. They seemed to think that self-esteem could be bought like a car or new clothes. Tom on the other hand did not want to pay the price required of him and masked his lack of self-confidence with false bravado and an exaggerated estimation of his athletic ability. If his team won Tom was quick to claim the glory, while if they lost he was sure some one else was to blame. The parents often encouraged this behavior, as Tom had become an extension of their own egos. They were sure that football was Tom's ticket to a college scholarship and that a professional football career was inevitable. Of course they were angry when Tom was benched by his coach for skipping practice and poor grades. The parents were certain that if Tom was not just allowed to play but to start, his self-esteem would be forever devastated. The parents threatened to sue the coach, the principal and the school board.

It is important to note that children develop self-esteem with our support and guidance, but if they are lacking in self-esteem they often require more adversity and discipline, not less.

Treating a child as though they are too fragile to succeed alone is one way to insure they don't succeed. In the situation above, Tom's parents actually contributed to his lack of self-esteem by contributing to his sense of grandiose self-importance.

"The Frantic Family Syndrome" is another reason that is often given as to why children are given special treatment. In the fast-paced world that we live in some parents say

"… it takes too much time and effort and I am so busy that this one time I will do this for my child. This is special."

Any working parent with a three-year-old knows that it is easier and quicker to tie the child's shoe than to wait for them to tie it. Of course, this practice presents some diminishing returns and loses its efficacy as the child ages. *Do you still tie your twenty-one year old son's shoe?* When parents take these short cuts they place more value on short-term results than long term benefits.

Upon examination the *good reason* is rarely good and often lacks reason when it is used to justify treating someone as special. The *good reason* is

just an excuse. The *good reason* is irresponsible and breeds dependency. Parents must remind themselves that their real goal is to help children become adults, and that there is no *good reason* for inhibiting this process.

THERE IS ALWAYS WASTEFULNESS AND AVARICE

How much is enough? How many Ninja turtles, Barbie dolls, Beanie Babies, Pokemon cards, TV's, computers, Playstations, Birkenstocks, Razor scooters or CD's does it take to satisfy the material lust of the **Fat Dog**.

"What does it take, to make my children happy," parents ask.

The answer, of course, is that things do not bring happiness, they only bring clutter. A basic truth in life is that *value is generally inversely related to quantity*. **Fat Dogs** value so little because they have so much. No matter how much a **Fat Dog** has, they always want more.

66

I have labeled this phenomenon the *"Terrible Too's"*, because **Fat Dogs** want too much. Like a toddler in the throes of the "terrible two's", the **Fat Dog** lives by the credo, **"I want what I want when I want it."** There is no differentiation here between *need* and *want* by the **Fat Dog**. Lest you think that this material accumulation is limited to the province of childhood, I once knew a middle aged **Fat Dog** who converted an entire bedroom into a closet for his two hundred rarely worn suits.

Much of the wastefulness derives from a distinct lack of impulse control coupled with a very short attention span. The **Fat Dog** revels in accumulation as an anxiety reduction mechanism, but despises the effort required for maintenance. Ultimately, the greatest wastefulness of the **Fat Dog** is their own potential.

The fear that they might fail is so great within them that they waste their life, being what they are rather than becoming what they might be.

THERE IS ALWAYS CYNICISM

A cynic is someone who attributes all actions to selfish motivations. The cynicism of the **Fat Dog** unmasks the charade played by the martyr. The parent martyr might say that they only want what is best for the **Fat Dog**, but they unwilling to let the **Fat Dog** fail for very selfish reasons ... personal parental pain. The **Fat Dog** is accurate when they whine that their parents do not love them enough, because ironically it is the parental self-centeredness that keeps them from letting their puppies go.

A true **Fat Dog** does not believe that they are loved unconditionally or that they deserve the love of others. They believe that the "gifts" from others and the special treatment that they receive are due to ulterior motives. **Fat Dogs** may expect to be treated as special, but they instinctively sense that there is some sort of catch. The **Fat Dog**, like a true cynic knows the cost of everything (though they expect someone else to pay it) and the value of very little. They do understand the value of avoiding pain or negative consequences, as this is constantly modeled and reinforced for them. **Fat Dogs** are like the Christians described by the apostle Paul who are "unwilling to accept the grace of (God's) love and are unwilling to seek salvation through good works."

The cyno-regressive view of the world is pessimistic in nature and rooted in the belief that people are unable to act in an altruistic manner. When a **Fat Dog** does a favor for someone, he is apt to perceive it not as a good deed but as a requisite of the reciprocity implicit in social exchange.

Because the motives of the Fat Dog are selfish, he believes that the motives of others are selfish also. The Fat Dog believes that everyone feels as worthless and as valueless as he does.

THE STATED GOAL OF THE PARENTS IS THE HAPPINESS OF THE CHILD

When I ask parents who bring their children to my office what they want, the usual reply is some variation of,

"We just want our baby to be HAPPY."

Parents who make such statements are usually not happy themselves and are looking for happiness in the wrong places, such as through their child's life. These parents possess a psychological immaturity and self-centeredness that severely limits their ability to think in a logical fashion. They often confuse momentary comfort with happiness. They do not want to suffer the pain of helping a child become an adult. In fact they may not really want their children to become adults, but they do want them to have the rewards and rights generally associated with adulthood. These parents do not understand that happiness, like life, often requires struggle and is a journey not a destination.

The most important goal of parenting can never be the short-term happiness of the child. It is illogical and arrogant to assume responsibility for the happiness of others and unethical to use the temporary pleasure of others as a balm for our own pain.

The most appropriate goal of parenting is to help children develop into independent and responsible adults.

If this goal is attained happiness is possible. If it is not attained despair is assured. A parent may give a **Fat Dog** many things (food, toys, second chances, praise, money and even love), but happiness is not one of them.

FAT DOGS DON'T PLAY

An old joke tells of a child who received the equivalent of a small toy store for Christmas, but that afternoon was found on the curb playing with all the empty toy boxes to the befuddlement of the parents. This story perfectly demonstrates the insatiable nature and resultant boredom inherent in the pathological puppy called a **Fat Dog.** After cajoling their parents into bankruptcy the **Fat Dog** tires of the Yuletide largesse and tries to find relief in the infinite creative possibilities of a simple cardboard box. Undoubtedly, the child will be rapidly chastised for not being happy, forced to leave the boxes on the curb and instructed to "spend more time with your things."

Older **Fat Dogs** acquire expensive toys (cars, boats, computers. houses, lovers, etc.), but have long forgotten how to enjoy them. Perhaps they never really learned how to play.

As they age Fat Dogs can't shake the feeling that everyone else is having more fun than they are or that they themselves could have fun if they could just find the perfect toy.

There are some **Fat Dogs** that confuse play with risk-taking and thrill- seeking. While these adrenaline junkies may actually have a brief glimpse of fun while nude nighttime skydiving over an active volcano, they have surpassed the bounds of healthy play in order to suppress their fears and anxieties. Of course, for the **Fat Dog,** it beats having to face the very real but mundane and less glamorous challenges of daily life most adults experience, such as paying the mortgage, holding a job and having a family.

Some **Fat Dogs** can't have fun because they turn most enjoyable opportunities for play into pseudo-work experiences. They say things like "If you want to play tennis with me then you need to work at it, I don't want any playing around."

Fat Dogs have difficulty perceiving play as an experience of pleasurable transcendent learning and continually corrupt it into an opportunity for ego magnification.

A slightly different example of this is the **Fat Dog** who becomes so enmeshed in games, that winning becomes an important prop to their ego.

Certainly, you have seen one of these Fat Dogs, decked-out in their teams colors, sitting in a sky-box and wailing like a banshee, because some eighteen year old *(who still loves to just play the game)*, with twenty-five thousand people screaming at him has missed a foul shot.

or

Perhaps you have witnessed a Fat Dog destroy a three hundred dollar tennis racket in a fit of rage.

or

Perhaps you have been awed by how far a Fat Dog can throw a five hundred-dollar driver when they can only hit a golf ball half that distance.

These super serious *players* do not deserve the appellation *ludi*, as their only interest in play is winning and by extension deriving a meaning for their existence. If they could play, or if they could remember what it was like to really play as a child they might glimpse at how play strengthens the ego without exaggerating the sense of self.

To play is to learn without fear.

THE FAMILY COMMUNICATES INDIRECTLY

A major problem often ascribed to dysfunctional families is the lack of communication. In the family of a

Fat Dog it may not be the lack of communication, but the method and content of communication that causes the most problems.

The most common methods of communication in these families are:

THREATS

DEMANDS

BARGAINING

SILENCE

The content is hard to discern at times because it is indirect and often expressed in a double bind or paradoxical manner. The content can generally be summarized as:

"YOU (THE FAT DOG) ARE STUPID, WORTHLESS, INADEQUATE AND TOTALLY INCAPABLE OF TAKING CARE OF YOURSELF, SO I (THE MARTYR) HAVE TO DO IT FOR YOU."

This message would be devastating enough if said openly and directly, but it gains much more power when it is covertly communicated by a parent's behavior (e.g. dressing a teenager, doing homework for a child or holding the bicycle too long). *How can the **Fat Dog** act like an adult when continually treated like a child?* There is a paradox and a double bind inherent when responding to such messages as, *"Act like an adult and do what you are told",* by a parent who is telling a child to turn in a paper that was written by the parent.

The **Fat Dog** experiences the indirect message of the martyr, internalizes the message and begins to believe it. This process breeds anger, frustration and distrust, all the while perpetuating the too feared failure.

There may not be a more efficient way to make some one hate you than to continually treat them as though they are stupid, worthless, inadequate and helpless.

For an example of this on a macro scale consider the emotional response some American foreign aid and social welfare programs have had on some developing countries. Better still; ask Native Americans about the impact of such messages on their people. Indeed, one of the most common arguments against affirmative action programs is that they perpetuate specialness and foster inadequacy. On a micro scale this type of communication is devastating to personal growth inside the family system. It is a wonder that **Fat Dogs** don't eat their parents. Perhaps this is what the Mennendez brothers had in mind.

PARENTAL RELATIONSHIPS ARE UNDERDEVELOPED

The one factor that has proven most effective over the years in predicting the development of a **Fat Dog** is the relationship between the parents. Indeed the one thing which might prove the most effective means of preventing the development of a **Fat Dog** is marital counseling or if possible pre-marital counseling. In most families that I have worked with, if there is a **Fat Dog,** the marital relationship has either never been very strong or has atrophied from lack of attention.

In these families, *the dependency of the Fat Dog is inversely related to the intimacy between the parents or the dependency of the Fat Dog increases as the connectiveness between the parents decreases.*

The marital relationship, often propped-up by the many trappings of success and privilege, may appear fine to the outside world. Unfortunately, both parents may be over-compensating as parents for their feelings of personal inadequacy and the emotional alienation they experience in the marriage.

- Both spouses generally feel they are carrying the whole load of the family by themselves.
- Both spouses generally feel undervalued and taken for granted.
- Both spouses often feel the one thing they thought marriage would protect them from...lonely.

These feelings are exacerbated when both spouses receive most of their ego-gratification in distinctly different venues. When both spouses work outside the home and focus their personal value on work the opportunity for this chasm increases exponentially.

These couples may initially gain a sense of worth from being perceived as "super parents"; who balance career, family and marriage with the ease of a juggler, and they may have difficulty seeing how their marital relationship negatively effects their children. Eventually, some of these parents develop a sub conscious wish to keep the **Fat Dog** in a state of permanent puppyhood in order to perpetuate the illusion of their own youth.

More often however, parental acts of overindulgence result from a lack of cohesive planning by parents who are afraid of confrontation. By focusing on the failures, needs, desires and inappropriate behavior of the **Fat Dog,** the spouses do not have to deal with their own issues. They can fight, rebel and even attempt to love through their child without the personal risks involved in an adult to adult relationship. As the **Fat Dog** becomes more an extension of the couple's relationship, the couple begins inappropriately investing in control of the child's destiny.

The long-term tragedy in such marriages is that the couple does not provide their children with a healthy model of adult to adult relationships. Instead they provide a picture of harried, narcissistic, neurotic psuedo-adults (such as the one's in most Woody Allen movies or TV sitcoms) for the child to mimic. The life of the child may provide a forum for the parents to meet in, but it can not nurture or sustain a marriage.

These couples are like vampires that are trying to absorb life from the child, instead of providing a marriage or family that can truly nurture the child.

Sometimes you can recognize these couples by the fact that they have numerous pictures of their children, but not their spouse in their wallet. They can recite verbatim things their children said years ago, but they can't remember what their spouse said last night.

Usually these marriages fall into a chasm of despair during the launching phase of the **Fat Dog,** and are at risk of total dissolution if their nest ever becomes truly empty. The lost opportunity for growth in the marital relationship that these parents forego while focusing on their child is the decay that causes the marital collapse. As their role as parents decreases these couples withdraw further from each other, afraid of interacting without a child to shield them. This is one reason some couples seem happy to have a forty year old **Fat Dog** still living in their home. *They need the eggs.*

Individual members of a **Fat Dog** family may come in great varieties but there seem to be certain general characteristics that are too common to be ascribed to chance. These characteristics are by no means exclusive and only represent patterns of behavior that are generally present. A quick glance at the list below may help explain why the marital relationship is so important and yet so underdeveloped in these families.

Fat Dog

Underachieving, unmotivated, self-centered, easily frustrated, emotionally labile, immature, cynical, angry, irresponsible, dependent and lazy

Siblings

Perfectionistic, high achieving, overcompensating, competitive, well mannered, quiet, likable and respectful.

Father

Successful, workaholic, emotionally distant, powerful, task-oriented, critical, hard driving, competitive and proud.

Mother

Perfectionistic, emotionally enmeshed, sensitive, fearful, creative, guilty, over-protective and proper.

Single Parent

Harried, guilty, overwhelmed, indecisive, self-sacrificing, timid, angry, over-involved and critical.

If the spouses in a marriage exhibit the above mentioned characteristics and they are dealing with family members that exhibit the above characteristics is there any doubt that their marriage would be in a state of atrophy. It is my contention that this atrophy is a primary contributor if not directly causal to the development of a **Fat Dog.**

THE FAT DOG HATES AND SHOWS DISRESPECT FOR THE PARENTS, AND THE PARENTS FEEL OVERWHELMED AND BETRAYED

By adolescence, defiance, hostility and a distinct surliness replaces the cute cuddly demeanor of the prepubescent **Fat Dog.** For many **Fat Dogs,** the first time they are brought to treatment is when they literally or metaphorically "bite the hand that feeds them." For many parents this act only verifies what they already fear in their hearts ... they are poor parents. The owner of the "bitten hand" is typically confused, hurt, angry and frustrated. These parents often moan over and over

"After all I have done for you... how could you do this?"

Perhaps one of the world's saddest sights is the pain and utter amazement in the eyes of the good-intended, but misguided parent who is reeling from a recent bout of viciousness by the **Fat Dog.** These parents may have many shortcomings, but their intent is generally benevolent and now they feel totally betrayed. Unfortunately, the more overprotective or overindulgent the parent has been and the more overprivileged the **Fat Dog** the more viscous the attacks can be. When these children finally explode, it is with the rage from years of pent-up hostility and inadequacy.

The disdain and disrespect that is heaped on these poor parents is much more obvious to individuals outside the family. Often family friends or relatives remark about this mistreatment, even when the enmeshed parents seem oblivious to it or powerless to confront it. In the animal world, when the proverbial hand bite occurs, the parent bites back. In the family of a **Fat Dog,** when the puppy bites one hand he is offered another one.

THE FAT DOG DISPLAYS SOCIAL DISINTEREST

When parents are confronted with chronic apathy and lack of motivation by the **Fat Dog**, they may push, prod, provoke or just whine, but they rarely see positive results. These parents often ask,

"How do I motivate my child, I have tried everything."

In fact they have not tried everything, and most often have been subverting the motivation of the **Fat Dog** by mediating the consequences of their actions. The **Fat Dog** seems not to care about any one or anything other than themselves. The parents feel helpless, defeated and double-crossed.

Questions that parents should be asking themselves, when confronted with unmotivated children, might include:

Why would anyone choose to worry, work, save or fret if someone else will do it for them?

What is the payoff that would entice the prince/princess to leave the castle and live in the forest (or even the suburbs)?

What am I doing to de-motivate this child?

Few of us can hope to leave the home of our parents and maintain the same standard of living. The impetus to leave must come from the realization that leaving is better than staying … or a strong parental push. A healthy young adult knows that their independence is worth the cost of the assumed responsibility and the risk of failure. **Fat Dogs** are afraid of failure and are willing to trade their independence for a sure thing.

For Fat Dogs puppyhood is desirable to doghood, *because* puppies don't have to care about anything or anyone else.

While the **Fat Dog** is wallowing in their narcissistic self-absorption, they are unable to develop what Alfred Adler called *Gemeinschaftsgefuhl* or *Social Interest.* The theory of *Social Interest* promotes the idea that contributing to the greater good of the community by an individual while learning to live in harmony with the community is a sign of personal maturity. This is congruent with such philosophies as:

"We should leave the world a better place than we found it. "

"Do unto others as you would have them do unto you. "

"It takes a village to raise a child. "

"From those to whom much is given much is expected.

The **Fat Dog** sees no utility in contributing to the greater good. He is not willing to "volunteer", "give back", "care about others" or "feed my sheep". You will only find a **Fat Dog** doing volunteer work if it is court ordered, or if there is something in it for themselves.The **Fat Dog** creates a world of *Social Disinterest, which* can best be described by the creeds:

"When I get <u>mine</u>, I don't care if you get yours, as long as it doesn't affect <u>me</u>."

and

"What's in this for <u>me</u>?"

or

"Why should I care?"

CHAPTER FIVE

WHAT MAKES A FAT DOG

"Those whom the gods wish to destroy, they first make powerful"

(with apologies to Euripides)

WHERE DO FAT DOGS COME FROM?

Many factors can contribute to the development of a **Fat Dog.**

These factors become significant only to the degree that they exaggerate normal parental tendencies toward overprivilege <u>and</u> impede the development of the child by chronically mediating the consequences of their narcissistic behavior.

These factors are *contributory* not *causal.* That means they may be *necessary, but not sufficient* to turn a child into a **Fat Dog.** There is no exclusive list of clearly contributory factors, and perhaps you can think of a few I have not, but for the purpose of this discussion I would suggest that the following be considered:

SOCIETAL CHANGE

CHILDHOOD TRAUMA OF THE PARENTS

PARENTAL TRAUMA IN ADULTHOOD

SUDDEN OVERWHELMING WEALTH OR POWER

SOCIETAL CHANGE

The last half of the last century has seen many changes throughout the entire world with the United States leading the way in reshaping modern society. Consider for a moment just a few of the changes that occurred in the last fifty years with direct consequences for parents and children in this country:

- The decrease in family size.
- The increase in expenditures on education.
- The increase in dual-career families.
- The increase in single-parent families.
- The increase in the length of childhood.
- The change in the value of children.
- An extended period of Peace and Prosperity.

Each of the above changes has effected the way we parent. It may be some time before we can discern the positive effects of these changes, but we can already distinguish some of the negative effects. One such development is a perceived increase in the number of **Fat Dogs.**

In just three generations the value of children in this country changed dramatically. As we rapidly moved from an agrarian society to a post-industrial society the economic value of children plummeted, but the concomitant decrease in family size made children more valuable as family standard bearers. My own family history exemplifies this quite well. All of my grandparents were born just prior to 1900 into large farming families. Both of my parents were born in the 1920's into families of nine plus children. My family of origin contained only three children, which was about average for mid-century. My current family has three children which is slightly above average for the end of the century. It is predicted that my children will each have only one or two children of their own.

I would not suggest that I love my children more than my great-grandparents loved my grandparents, I am only suggesting that quantity does have a relationship to value. My great-grandparents needed children to survive economically, but with nine children the loss of a child may not have had the same effect it might in a family with only two children. Today children rarely are economic assets to the family and are generally economic liabilities, but they are treated like princes/princesses.

The explosion of dual-career and single-parent families during the last fifty years has had a major impact on parenting in the United States. These "nontraditional" families are not inherently evil, inadequate or incapable of providing appropriate parenting. However, like an one-legged horse in a steeplechase they are at a distinct disadvantage. I once suggested, tongue-in-cheek, that in order to have children families should be required to have three adults. My statement was based on the logic that it seemed to take two incomes and a full-time caregiver to sustain and nurture a family in modern America. Todate my suggestion has not gained much support, but I constantly meet frustrated, overwhelmed and exhausted individuals who say they need more help to raise their family.

In an ideal world both parents would be easily accessible and perpetually available, like Ward and June Cleaver. Unfortunately, modern America seems to value self-expression, consumption and career more than parenting.

In modern families parenting resources are stretched thin, overwhelming the parents and leaving them so short on time that they seek the most expedient methods of parenting. Modern parents are more likely to "do for" their children, feel guilty about the constraints of time on their interactions and overprivilege their children into **Fat Dogs.**

Consider how the growth in the number of single-parent families has complicated the situation. Single parents often have no choice about working outside of the home and parenting on the run. Single parents often may seem to have no choice but to leave large amounts of parenting to others (e.g. teachers, coaches, friends and even other children). Single parents often not only have to shoulder the financial and care-giving responsibilities of the family, but they may also carry the baggage of a failed relationship. These parents often become martyrs, never fully develop their own potential and deprive their children of a healthy adult role model. The guilt, frustration, lack of resources and emotional enmeshment of the single parent puts them at risk for contributing to the development of a **Fat Dog.**

Let's be clear that being a single parent or having a dual-career family is not enough to cause a **Fat Dog.** Indeed well adjusted adults can come from these types of families. These families are dysfunctional only to the extent that the parents become so overwhelmed, insecure, distracted or paralyzed by guilt that they stop being parents.

Along with the "baby boom" and the rapid changes in the structure of the family came the development of *Parenting Science.* Few books have ever had the impact on a society as Dr. Benjamin Spock's, <u>Baby and Child Care.</u> It can be argued whether this is a fine and useful book, but it is undeniable that to the generations of parents who read it, this book suggested that there was a science to correct parenting. Today, what profitable bookstore does not have several shelves of parenting books? Every "baby boomer" must have several parenting books (check your shelves, I have over twenty parenting books). Even the best of these authors, offer little to their readers that has not been common knowledge for generations. For the most part these books exhort readers to quit being irresponsible and start parenting like an adult and not a scared child. The paradox is that even with this plethora of "new information on how to parent", parents feel less than adequate.

Parenting Science has not made us better parents, instead it has contributed to our fear that everyone else knows something that we don't and if we could just learn it everything would be okay. The truth is that being a good parent is hard work, and almost as unique an experience as growing from childhood to adult.

CHILDHOOD TRAUMA OF PARENTS

Wordsworth's statement that "the child is the father to man", reminds us that the one thing all parents have in common is that they have been children and as such bring the experiential baggage of childhood with them into adulthood.

Sometimes a **Fat Dog** may trace its genesis to some transgenerational trauma, which occurred years before their birth. Transgenerational traumas are traumas that occur in one generation but through adaptation or compensation becomes fulminate in another generation. These traumas can be personal (e.g. mental illness) or more general societal traumas (e.g. the Great Depression), but each can effect future generations.

Personal childhood trauma can range from active physical abuse to neglect. Another type of trauma in this category is the loss of a parent through death, divorce or pre-occupation. This type of injury to a child can caused them to be injured adults and inadequate parents, thus causing a **Fat Dog** in the next generation when the parent tries to compensate for their own injury. For example, a child who has been sexually abused may fear their own ability to nurture as an adult and may compensate by over-nurturing as a parent. It can be very difficult to model appropriate parent-child relationships, if you did not experience them as a child first.

Societal trauma, war for example, can effect whole generations and impact the way they parent. My favorite example of this is what has been called the "Great Depression Syndrome." The parents of my co-horts were mostly children during the "Great Depression" (1929-1939), and as a result endured poverty and tribulation. It seems that everyone lived at least ten miles from anywhere and it snowed for the entire decade while they all hovered around that single piece of glowing coal in the hearth, eating cold cornmeal mush. Many of the survivors of the "Great Depression" developed a self-confidence born of ingenuity and self-reliance in the face of necessity. They became self-motivated to survive as a result of hardship and privation. As adults members of this hardworking go-getter generation were often heard to say things such as,

"I just want my kids to have it easier than I did",

or

'No child of mine will ever have to do the things I did."

These well-meaning parents had been traumatized by the "Great Depression" and they went to great lengths to ensure that their children did not suffer the same experiences. Some of these "Great Depression" heroes went overboard, and in a great rush of survivor guilt overprivileged their children.

Why were they surprised when their children turned out different from them?

and

Why were they so surprised that many of their children turned out to be spoiled, self-absorbed, self-centered incompetents?

I am not suggesting that these parents should have forced their children to walk to school barefoot in the snow to instill self-reliance. I am suggesting that parents should be careful about mediating the experiences of their children. We all become what we are. *Fat Dogs are a result of excess, even when it appears well intended.*

PARENTAL TRAUMA IN ADULTHOOD

There are times when healthy well-adjusted children grow-up to be healthy well-adjusted adults, yet their ability to parent becomes impaired. This impairment is usually the result of a trauma sustained as an adult. The trauma may be personal such as a chronic illness or it may be relationship based such as a bitter divorce. Even healthy adults are vulnerable to parental impairment if the trauma they sustain is the death, illness or disability of one of their children.

It is easy to understand how a personal impairment in adulthood, such as addiction or chronic mental/physical illness would impact an individual ability to parent.

- Addicts often become overindulgent to conceal their own guilt.
- Individuals suffering from heart disease or rape victims might become overprotective.
- The erratic moods of a parent with Bi-polar disorder make it difficult for them to set consistent boundaries.

Relationship problems affecting parenting are generally a result of unhealthy adult-to-adult relationships through divorce, co-dependency or even widowhood. This occurs when the lack of healthy adult-to adult relationship leave the parent feeling overwhelmed. This problem is further exacerbated if the parent begins over-relating with the child. Such a parent would seek ego-gratification and support from the child, making it almost impossible for the parent to set appropriate boundaries for the child.

Even healthy adults in healthy relationships are not immune to the trauma of losing a child or having a child

99

with special needs. Having a child die can makes the overprotection and overindulgence of other children in the family seem rational. This behavior is fueled by the two-headed psychological monster, "Limiting-future-loss" and "What-might-have-been". The surviving children are at great risk to become **Fat Dogs.**

SUDDEN OVERWHELMING WEALTH OR POWER

Perhaps we would all share with Icarus the desire to fly too high and too fast if we were suddenly given the power of flight. If so we would just as surely share his fate. Perhaps we all would, like Daedelus, give wings to our children if we could. If so, just as surely we would share his fate. It takes time to soar like an eagle.

Are we willing to invest the necessary time to teach our children to fly*?*

Most of the **Fat Dogs** I have known are the children of very successful people. The parents, mostly from solid working-class backgrounds, rarely knew wealth or privilege as a child, yet became successful doctors, lawyers, business executives, politicians, entertainers, etc. Through hard work, luck, perseverance, wise choices and sacrifices these individuals accumulated wealth/power quickly. Unfortunately, these otherwise very disciplined and intelligent people lavished their largesse on their children. Whether this bounty was bestowed out of guilt, convenience, misguided beneficence or ignorance the resultant ruin was easy to predict. The newly minted **Fat Dog** will exhibit an increased sense of entitlement and a decreased sense of self-worth and motivation. The parents have perverted the old adage, "those to whom much is given much is expected" and reframed it to, "those to whom too much is given, little is expected."

Power and wealth are not intrinsically evil, but we must always remember that even though they are not always earned they always have a cost.

Perhaps this is what Jesus was really addressing when he said," it is easier for a camel to pass through the eye of a needle than for a rich man to pass into heaven."

Often the people who earn the power and wealth think they can bestow them on the next generation. Mostly this ends in disaster for the next generation and perhaps many generations thereafter as they pay the cost.

How many times is the drama of "shirtsleeves to shirtsleeves in three generation" or "clogs to clogs in three generations" been played-out?

How many times do parents aid in the destruction of their own children by trying to give them what must be earned?

King Lear displays eloquently the tragedy that ensues when a powerful father tries to foolishly divest his power to his children without adequate preparation. The Fool's chastisement of Lear rings true and should be heeded by all..." You should be beaten for being old before being wise." What a great research project the second and third generations of the Silicon Valley and Dot.Com wealth explosion should make. Already the high-pitched whine of **Fat Dogs** echo through the valley.

CHAPTER SIX

HOW TO MAKE A FAT DOG RUN

MAKING A FAT DOG RUN

So, you have read this far and you are beginning to realize that the thirty-five year old adolescent living in your basement, who has not had a job since Reagan was president but has a great tan, might be a **Fat Dog.** You find yourself angered by your puppy's behavior and embarrassed by their passivity, but you still do not believe that they can survive in the real world alone. You are aware that your **Fat Dog** is growing more indolent, less motivated and angrier with you every day.

How can you make this Fat Dog run? Read on.

Please note that the state of being a **Fat Dog** is not a normal state of adolescent development and thus requires unusual and somewhat extreme responses. All of these suggestions are meant to comply with the basic law of inertia ("a body at rest will remain at rest until acted upon by an overwhelming force") and to cause movement in the **Fat Dog.**

The more extreme and severe suggestions are not meant for normal adolescents and their parents.

The basic steps in making a **Fat Dog** run are listed below:

> **Step One: Improve your Marital Relationship**
> **Step Two: Establish Sound Parenting Goals**
> **Step Three: Remember What Worked for You**
> **Step Four: Let Go of the Bicycle**
> **Step Five: Starve the Puppy**

These steps are meant to be taken in order and to build on each other. As parents proceed through the steps there should be discernible movement on the part of the **Fat Dog.** As they say in 12-step groups, "half measures avail us nothing", so the steps must be consistent and continuous. The **Fat Dog** must be convinced that the parents really mean business and that life as they knew it is changing. Only in extreme cases should parents have to proceed to the final step, but when they take the first step they must be prepared to take the last step.

STEP ONE: IMPROVE THE MARITAL RELATIONSHIP

If you are going to overcome the inertia of a **Fat Dog** at rest you will need plenty of support. Start by improving your primary support system ... your marriage. The marriage is the most important relationship in the family because:

The primary relationship in any family is between the spouses.

If the marital relationship is not nurtured and sustained it is doubtful any other relationship in the family can aspire to health. In helping a child make the transition to adulthood it is doubly important to model a healthy adult-to-adult relationship like the one found in a healthy marriage.

Parents of **Fat Dogs** must be aware of their needs as individuals, part of a couple or as a member of the family and strive to get them met. If you are not sure your marriage is healthy or that your needs are getting adequately met in the relationship refer to the list below of characteristics commonly associated with healthy marital relationships.

- **Individual growth is encouraged and rewarded.**
- **The spouses are interdependent and not co-dependent.**
- **Decision-making for the most part is collaborative.**
- **The couple has regular time together and occasionally exclusively couple time apart from the family.**
- **Marital relationship issues are not worked out through the children.**
- **Each spouse believes the other would always intend him or her well not ill.**
- **All things being equal, when given a choice, spouses choose the company of each other.**
- **Communication between spouses is respectful, honest and direct.**

Humans are social animals and generally choose not to be alone.

Adults form units in all cultures not just to promote survival of the species, but to *allow for optimal personal growth.*

If you and your spouse can improve your marriage, you will also grow as individuals and model a more healthy relationship for the **Fat Dog.**

One telltale sign that the marital relationship is improving is that the Fat Dog will no longer be the center of family concern.

If the marriage flourishes and the **Fat Dog** fails or perishes, the family will be much better equipped to deal with the pain or loss.

Single parents should note that this reasoning means their world should no longer be child- entered either. The single parent's health needs (including relationship needs) must be met before the **Fat Dog** can progress.

An example of why this is necessary is the airlines' in-flight instruction that warns, "parents flying with small children should place the oxygen mask over their own face <u>first </u>in the event of an emergency." Even super-parents are of little help to their children if they are not breathing.

If the single parent is going to mobilize a **Fat Dog** they must first mobilize themselves, and where appropriate develop more healthy adult-to-adult relationships. It is not impossible for a single parent to help a **Fat Dog** become an adult; it is just much harder to do this alone.

In twenty-five years as a therapist, I have never seen a marriage that did not need improvement if there was a **Fat Dog** present in the family. Also I have never met a healthy single parent who had a **Fat Dog** as a child. Healthy marriages make parenting easier because it fosters healthy adults. Healthy adults, either singularly or as part of a marriage, not only are capable of modeling healthy behavior, but also are more able to set appropriate limits for their children.

STEP TWO: ESTABLISH PARENTING GOALS

Usually parents can't make their **Fat Dog** run because they have forgotten or never knew what constituted appropriate goals for parenting. Just as it is important to know where you are going to have a successful trip, it is important to know what your goals are to raise a child successfully. Unfortunately, many parents give very little thought to what appropriate parenting goals should be. For the most part the parents of a **Fat Dog** believe that their child's short-term happiness is the only goal they need. The child usually sees through this charade and realizes that their parents are actually only interested in maintaining their own comfort level. What results from the ensuing struggle is that neither child nor parents achieve the goals they have espoused.

In an attempt to stimulate discussion and thought on what appropriate parenting goals should be I have listed below a set of goals which I believe will not only make a **Fat Dog** run, but if implemented early enough might prevent the development of a **Fat Dog.**

The first goal of parenting is to help children become independent and responsible adults.

The second goal of parenting is to help children become altruistic and compassionate.

The third goal of parenting is to help children develop rational thinking skills.

The fourth goal of parenting is the transgenerational inculcation of values.

The fifth goal of parenting is to help the species not just survive but to flourish.

Parents may reject or accept these goals as appropriate for their family, what is important is that they establish some goals. The operationalization of these goals must be worked out by parents in each generation with the realization that each generation may be the last of that family. It is essential that these goals be incorporated into

111

family traditions, rituals and daily life. For example in order to operationalize the first goal of parenting (as stated above) a child may be given a regular family maintenance task that is developmentally appropriate and thus receives concomitant freedoms:

A first grader feeds the pets or clears the table each evening and is allowed to extend their bedtime to 8:30 PM on school nights.

A middle-schooler prepares dinner for the family once a week and is allowed to shop unsupervised at the mall.

Children must find that freedom is earned or they will never value it and develop the courage to enjoy it.

In attempting to attain parenting goals, parents should never underestimate the power of institutions (schools, churches, etc.), organizations (scouts, clubs, etc.), activities (soccer, baseball, dance, drama. etc.) and people (family, friends, peers, teachers, etc.) in helping reinforce these goals. The importance of how these goals can be reinforced by others was revealed to my wife and I several years ago when our teenage daughter spent several weeks at a wilderness camp. This experience (an ordeal with strangers) crystallized much of what we had to try to teach our daughter and reinforced the goals of self-reliance and responsibility in ways that we could not have achieved alone.

Don't be too proud to let others help in preventing the development of a Fat Dog. Let others help. If necessary get professional help.

*Remember the three **R's** ...Review, Reinforce, and Reinforcements.*

REVIEW *your parenting goals regularly.*

REINFORCE *the behavior you want.*

REINFORCEMENTS *can help. You don't have to parent alone.*

STEP THREE: REMEMBER WHAT WORKED FOR YOU

When parents lament that their **Fat Dog** is out of control and they do not know how to correct the situation, I ask them to tell me what experiences shaped their own development and contributed to them becoming independent responsible adults. Many of these successful adults have a poignant story, which includes childhood poverty, depravation or loss. Many tell of real hunger, unsavory jobs, numbing schedules and even abject failure. Each of these parents had some story of what "lit the fire in their belly", with a hunger that helped them overcome adversity. In the same breath most of these parents go on to tell me that they do not want their children to struggle this way or that they want a <u>better</u> life for their children.

Better? What is better about being deprived of an opportunity to become independent and responsible.

I agree with Dizzy Dean, "You got to dance with who brung you." If hard work, sacrifice, persistence and simplicity helped the parents become successful adults, why would they not be good for the next generation?

The core question here is "How do we learn" or more directly, "How do we learn to be who we are?" If we are not one of the fortunate few who seem to spring from their mother's womb "knowing" who they are, we must some how learn how to be who we are. Do we learn best by listening, watching, thinking or doing? Certainly we must employ all of the above methods of learning, but the parents of **Fat Dogs** seem to underestimate the value of doing. They assume that knowledge is somehow passed from generation to generation via telepathy or osmosis. Perhaps this explains the popularity of "reality show on TV," their fans think that somehow they will "learn" about life by watching reel people (actors, mostly very poorly trained) in reel situations (dramas concocted for viewing audiences), instead of experiencing real life themselves.

Can you imagine the results if you only *told* your child how to ride a bicycle, or only let the child *watch* you ride a bike, or only *read* a book about how to ride a bike. In order to master riding a bike the child must develop a sense of balance and risk many falls, both of which can only be done by doing something. In order to become an accomplished biker you must become a failed biker or at least someone who risks failing as a biker.

If you have a **Fat Dog** remember that they must experience freedom, failure and accountability if they are to become adults.

Parents should examine what experiences helped them develop into adults and seek to provide similar opportunities for their children.

This doesn't mean that if a parent went to work in the coal mines at the age of ten that they should send their ten-year-olds into the mine. What I am suggesting is that, if you have a late stage adolescent that is not thriving, try offering them opportunities similar to the ones that shaped your own development.

The urban environment that most Americans live in doesn't offer the opportunities experienced just one or two generations ago by most children to contribute daily to the survival of their family. I am not saying that there are no **Fat Dogs** in rural areas, I am just observing that urban life does not offer as many natural opportunities for children to contribute and *do*. This is one of the reasons the programs like Outward Bound and farm camps have been so successful.

It has been my pleasure and good fortune to have several of my **Fat Dogs** taken in by Mennonite farm families for periods ranging from several weeks to months. The simple, honest, respectful, devout, hard-working Mennonites almost always succeed in helping **Fat Dogs** act like adults, even when overindulgent parents and therapists have failed miserably. The Mennonites are not afraid that the **Fat Dog** will fail, because they have great faith and they believe in the value of their lifestyle. They make few demands, but their expectations are clear and congruently modeled.

STEP FOUR: LET GO OF THE BICYCLE

When I was eighteen I left the comfort of my rural home for the more sophisticated and uncharted territory of Chapel Hill, North Carolina. A very remarkable thing happened on that beautiful fall afternoon. The parents who had loved, protected, nurtured and defended me for almost two decades …

LET ME GO!!!

In retrospect, I know that it must have been very difficult for my parents to let me go. Not only was I the first born and the first person in the family to go to college, but I had been born prematurely with a birth defect and my parents had lost a second child through a full-term miscarriage. According to my siblings I was certainly my parents favorite child. My parents had lots of *good reasons* to overprotect and overindulge me, but they

LET ME GO!!!

Theirs was an act of real love. I hope that when the time comes, I can demonstrate my love for my children with as much grace as my parents did.

When parents bring their **Fat Dogs** to my office they are in so much pain and anguish it is difficult believe that things could be worse. In the minds of these parents what is worse is the *feeling of helplessness* they ascribe to letting their children go. The parent's abject fear is fueled by the fear of the image of their **Fat Dog** failing and the parent's own sense of not being able to bear the pain. The **Fat Dog** is both fearful and rebellious (they want to fly but are afraid of heights). The battle of fears that develops can keep the **Fat Dog** immobile for years. If the parent's fears win then the child will always remain a child. If the fears of the child wins out then the result may well be the same.

Children become adults by developing the courage to face their fears. Parents are not truly adults until they face their fears about their children.

The parents of **Fat Dogs** are so fearful that they can't

LET THEIR CHILDREN GO.

Earlier I used the metaphor of teaching a child to ride a bicycle as an example of appropriate parenting. Parents who have successfully taught a child to ride a bike can appreciate the poem below. Parents who have not taught a child to ride a bike or the parents of **Fat Dogs** might learn even more.

THE LESSON

If you live your life through them
If you have cared and cared and cared
If you meet their every whim

If your tears seem never dry
If you always wonder why

If you're sorry they you sired
If you fear a living death

If your legs and lungs are tired
If you have just one more breath

LET GO OF THE BICYCLE!!!

If you recognize yourself in this poem, but are still having difficulty letting go of the bike, you can always start by installing training wheels. As long as the child is doing most of the work progress is possible.

STEP FIVE: STARVE THE PUPPY

At the beginning of this book I warned that it was not meant for everyone and that most parent-child relationships were not as extreme as the **Fat Dog** syndrome. The methods described here should not be applied indiscriminately to child raising. However, if you recognize that you have a **Fat Dog** and you have tried everything else to no avail, then you have an *extreme case,* and it might call for *extreme measures, much like the strategies suggested by the group Toughlove.* If you have an extreme case I would suggest two things:

- **DON'T CONTRIBUTE TO THE PROBLEM**. I am just repeating this because this is the most important step. It requires that you first review your own behavior and eliminate any actions which mediate the consequences of the **Fat Dog's** behavior or rewards their amotivation.

- **STARVE THE PUPPY**. This is an extreme measure and not to be taken without thorough planning nor is it to be committed to half-heartedly. This action requires firmly and consistently cutting the **Fat Dog's** end of the family dinner table off: no food, no housing, no money … toughlove.

The idea of starving the puppy might seem radical. It is radical. If what you have been doing hasn't worked doing it longer or harder probably won't work either, it is time to try something different. If you have ever observed a mother dog weaning her pups you can understand how necessary this unpleasantness is.

Remember, the mother dog is not deterred in her duty by being called a bitch.

Just picture the she-dog snarling, barking, biting and running away from her young, until the starving puppies learn to feed themselves. She counts on the drive to survive and hunger to motivate her little ones as they overcome their dependency; can you imagine what would happen if she gave in to their incessant whining and relentless pressure to be fed? Now can you imagine what will happen if you do not starve your puppy?

Although I have never observed it I have been told that the bald eagle has a similar training process for baby eaglets. When the adult eagles think it is time for the fledglings to fly they stop feeding them. To speed up the process the adult eagles roost on a nearby branch and eat while their young scream and starve a few feet away. Eventually the hungry baby birds leap out of the nest and fly to the food, risking certain death if they fail. Some fail, the rest learn to fly.

The weaning process is one of survival. It is also a process of love and respect, but not necessarily tenderness. If you have a **Fat Dog** you already know that tenderness alone does not always work. Although the **Fat Dog** might whine, snarl, beg or bite you must be firm.

Remember, cutting the puppy off from your dependence is actually a vote of confidence.

Anytime you decrease the dependence on of a child you are saying to the **Fat Dog,** "I know you will not let yourself starve and I believe you have the wherewithal to survive and eventually flourish." This is a replication of the message Adam and Eve got at the gates of Eden. Keep the faith.

CHAPTER SEVEN

HOW TO PREVENT A FAT DOG

*Courage, an optimistic attitude, common sense, and a feeling of being at home upon
the crust of the earth, will enable (us) to face advantages and disadvantages with
equal firmness.*
Alfred Adler

CAN WE PREVENT FAT DOGS?

You may be beginning to wonder if there is any more hope of preventing your beautiful child from becoming a **Fat Dog** than there is of preventing fire ants from taking over the world. Certainly there is hope (unfortunately not in the case of stopping the fire ants), because

> **even though humans start life as self-centered, helpless and dependent, most people find that their personal survival is best served by not just caring for themselves but caring for others too.**

Most children find independence and responsibility self-rewarding and unless hampered will eventually become adults. The following are my reflections on what strategies might prevent the development of **Fat Dogs** under normal circumstances. If you are afraid you might be currently contributing to the development of a nascent **Fat Dog** read on.

DON'T HAVE CHILDREN

The above is not meant to be a flippant statement. Experience has proven that many **Fat Dogs** started as puppies of people who should not be breeding. Without trying to determine who should have children and who should not, I am merely suggesting that couples take this decision seriously.

If you do not think you can love children enough to be a good parent, don't have children.

Many people think that they are suppose to have children and that parenting is suppose to be easy. *It is not easy to be a good parent.* Other than a biological imperative to continue the species parents who want parenting to be easy have little need to reproduce, although they may want to reproduce for many reasons.

If adults believe that they can not perform the duties of a good parent, then it is an act of selfless rational thought to remain childless. If on the other hand these individuals are tethered to selfish whims then they should heed the warning of Sir Francis Bacon,

"... to take a spouse and have children is to give hostages to fortune."

Not only does being a good parent require hard work, it can invite great emotional pain. Actively choosing not to be a parent requires a keen awareness of one's ability and willingness to accept responsibility for one's behavior. **Fat Dogs** may be more a product of training than genes, but one clear way to stop their development is to not start it. If you do not want a **Fat Dog** one clear option is to not have children.

Some of my friends and acquaintances have chosen to remain childless, ruling out even adoption, because they are afraid children would change their lives. They are right; having children would definitely change their lives. While I mourn the loss these friends will experience, I applaud their decision because many of them would indeed breed **Fat Dogs.**

LOVE YOUR CHILDREN

In Corinthians 1:13:13 the apostle Paul says that love is the greatest of all attributes. Certainly much evil has been done in the name of love, but love is the answer. If you do not wish to create a **Fat Dog** you must love your child. Most parents would assert that they do love their children and I would agree, but I might question how they operationalize their love. Consider the following:

- Loving your child does not mean protecting them from the bogeyman under their bed. **Loving your child means standing with your child in the darkness of their fears so that they can learn the courage to confront fear.**

- Loving your child does not mean giving them everything that they want. **Loving your child means actively attempting to give your child what they need. Most often what they need is to be loved.**

- Loving your child does not make them perfect children. **Loving your child means accepting the imperfections and failures required to become a healthy adult.**

- Loving your child does not mean only teaching your child how to survive. **Loving your child means teaching your child how to flourish.**

- Loving your child does not mean holding them close to your heart. **Loving your child means letting them go so they can find <u>their</u> way home.**

- Loving your child does not mean loving them for what they could be. **Loving your child means loving them for who they are.**

Let your love be visible in your actions and audible in your words. Praise, encourage and lead your children. Teach your children to love and forgive themselves, by loving and forgiving them. Let them see that your love is unconditional and complete even in the face of misbehavior.

It is important to remember that the word *compassion* derives from a Latin phrase meaning, "to go with" not "to go for", and thus we should *suffer with* not *suffer for* our children.

Children will push limits in order to find them and the security that comes from knowing them.

Love your children by setting boundaries, expectations and limits for your children while they are learning to do this for themselves. Remember that the boundaries and expectations must continue to grow as the child grows or the boundaries will limit the child's growth. Can you imagine the consequences of forcing a teenager to wear diapers in order so that they might not soil themselves?

If you love your children in the ways stated above, they will *believe* that they are loved, and real *Fat Dogs* never believe that they are loved or that they are lovable.

<u>FOCUS ON NEED NOT WANTS</u>

One of life's most difficult tasks is determining the difference between needs and wants. The United States is a country of enormous wealth, yet there are pockets of poverty and a disturbing amount of wastefulness. Our consumer culture has equated wants with needs, confused rights with entitlements, and left even the very wealthy feeling impoverished. Parents must teach children at an early age that all impulses are not equal and that some impulses are harmful. If parents are successful at this task then the likelihood of raising a **Fat Dog** is greatly diminished.

Once during a lecture I commented that no one *needed* a pair of $150 sneakers. An attractive young woman raised her hand and said that I was wrong. She revealed that her husband was a sales representative for a well-known brand of sneakers and she was certain everyone needed a pair of $150 sneakers. Perhaps she was right as this applied to her family finances. I still contend that wanting to be shod like Michael Jordan is not the same thing as *needing* to be shod like Michael

Jordan. I suppose there is nothing wrong with wanting to play basketball like Mr. Jordan, but since no one else has been able to I don't see how this can be a *need*.

Children do *need*

    love,

      security,

        boundaries

        sustenance

          and stability in order to develop.

Children do not *need* _____ (you fill-in the blank).

It is not important that the spoon, which carries oatmeal to a child's mouth, is silver or plastic, it is only important that the spoon is functional and that the child can eat. Children often understand the difference between wants and *needs* better than their parents, realizing that too often *their own wants are little more than the projected wants of their parents.* I am not too proud to admit that my son (like his father before him) would often rather play with a stick he found in the yard than most of the toys he said he *needed.*

If you do not wish to have a **Fat Dog**, focus on meeting the *needs* of your children and do not waste time, energy or sleep with concern about their wants. If the want is truly important to the child they can work towards its attainment on their own.

REMEMBER THAT YOUR PRIMARY GOAL AS A PARENT IS TO HELP YOUR CHILD BECOME AN INDEPENDENT RESPONSIBLE ADULT

Many parents forget that their primary goal is to work themselves out of a job. Instead they try to insure the short-term happiness of their children. These parents actively seek the approval of their children and are fond of saying things like,

"I want to be my daughter's best friend."

As a result these parents are prone to make poor parenting decisions, while missing untold opportunities to help their children become adults.

If your primary goal is *to aid your child in becoming an independent responsible adult* which of the following would be most important:

Your child making the honor role every year

or

Your child mastering the learning process

Your child winning 1st prize at a science fair with your help

Or

Your child getting no ribbon, but doing their own work

Your child cleaning their room every time you tell them to

Or

Your child cleaning their room

Your child following all the rules

Or

Your child doing what is right

Your child always getting what they want

Or

Your child getting mostly what they need

Your child liking you

Or

Your child knowing what their boundaries are

Generally we don't couch choices into the options above, that was done just to make you realize that our choices as parents do have consequences that are sometimes shaped by what we didn't actively choose.

If your child has to struggle, risk, suffer and sometimes be unhappy, then perhaps they can become adults and not Fat Dogs.

Parents must continually remember that their primary goal is to *help their children become independent responsible adults.*

Below is a true story of how one mother, without the benefit of parent education classes and the advice of experts operationalized her goal as a parent.

Frying Bacon

When I was nine years old my mother decided to teach me how to cook. She did this by refusing to stop picking strawberries and give-in to my plaintive pleas of imminent starvation. She said that a boy my age was certainly old enough to fry bacon. She then gave me brief instructions on how to fry bacon and said that she would be in to check on me in a few minutes. In the spirit of passive-aggressive nine-year-olds everywhere, I threw a pound of bacon into a cast iron skillet and cranked the gas range up to high. I then loudly suffered sizzling pork grease on my tender naked flesh. My mother calmly entered the kitchen with a bucket of strawberries and a smile. She slowly cut down the gas, handed me a towel and then sat down at the table with a cup of coffee. Next she carefully explained to me that the laws of thermodynamics necessitated that bacon be fried *more slowly and in a lesser quantity than I had attempted if tragedy was to be averted. Finally, she added that <u>her</u> kitchen had two basic rules, which must be obeyed at all times and by all people:*

Rule 1: You mess it up, you clean it up.

Rule 2: You cook it, you eat it.

As she walked out of the kitchen she said I had done well for my first attempt and could now cook for myself whenever I was hungry. I ate that whole pound of deep-fat fried bacon and cleaned-up the kitchen. I never forgot.

<u>EXPECT SUCCESS BUT ALLOW FOR FAILURE</u>

Failure is greatly misunderstood and underrated. It can strengthen, motivate and transform a person like little else. Many parents are failure phobic, because they live through their children and any failure by the child exacerbates the inadequacies of the parent. A wise man once told me, "Anything worth doing … is worth doing poorly … at first."

If a child is too fearful of failure they are unlikely to risk learning new or difficult skills. If a parent is too fearful of the child's failure they will continually intercede, and the child will never know whether or not they can succeed on their own.

These parents need to let go of the bicycle.

Unfortunately, some parents expect very little of their children, and what they do expect is often negative. Often these parents say things like,

"I don't want to rob my child of their childhood. I don't want them to grow-up too fast."

It is important to have high expectations for ourselves and our children, and as suggested in the often-cited Pygmalion effect, people often behave in response to the way they are treated. Each generation should be expected to leave the world a little better than they found it. Each child should be expected to contribute to the family, not diminish it.

We must *expect* our children to become independent and responsible adults if they are to believe that they can, but we must accept that there may be many small failures along the way.

<u>MODEL YOUR VALUES</u>

Perhaps we have no choice but to model our values, if our values are nothing more than our personal beliefs that we actuate. If you do not live your beliefs, they just remain beliefs and never become values. What I am suggesting is that parents strive for congruence between the beliefs that they espouse and the actions of their daily life. If you believe that children should become independent responsible adults, show them what one looks like by modeling values which are congruent.

Make rational decisions

Accept responsibility for your life

Deal with the consequences of your actions

Do the right thing

Be loving

Care about others

Be respectful

Look for beauty

Take risks

Accept happiness

Eat your vegetables

Do unto others, as you would have them do unto you

Listen more, talk less

Forgive your own foolishness

Play

Tell the truth

Pray for your enemies

Don't eat the seed corn

Cry, Laugh and Dance

Never give up

ACCEPT THAT LEARNING IS AN EXPERIENTIAL PROCESS

Children, like adults, learn best by *doing*, let them *do* as much as possible. So much emphasis has been placed on formal education during the last fifty years, that we forget that school is an artificial experience created to foster and communicate acquired knowledge. For the most part the knowledge acquired in a school is meaningless unless applied or experienced beyond the realm of academia. There is a saying attributed to Plato that says,

"we must educate the rich, because the poor will learn what they need to know."

The implication is that without the motivation of survival the rich would have to learn through artificial means ... a school for fools.

There was a time when survival skills had to be practiced as part of daily life, even by the wealthiest members of society, but today this is no longer true for most people. Today children do not have as many opportunities to *do,* as they have to watch and listen.

Process implies the possibility of incremental and at times slow steps. People learn over a period of time and real change can proceed at a pace that makes snails appear jet-propelled. Often parents want to speed up the development of their children and mistakenly think that this is good (Piaget thought that this was a distinctly American trait). Just as often these parents offer little tolerance for their children growing at their own pace. My advice is, do not despair, glaciers might move slowly but they do move. One of my colleagues tells the story of his own mother, who while complaining about some childish indiscretion on his part ended her diatribe with,

"and look how you have turned out."

To which my colleague's stepfather wisely retorted,

"Martha, I'm not sure the boy is through turning out."

If your child falters do not be disheartened, they may not be *through turning out yet.*

The true **Fat Dog** consistently seems to be a helpless, needful self-centered, unmotivated leech. They are denied the opportunity to learn from experience because some one else mediates the consequences of their failures and exaggerates their successes. If this is to be prevented the process will require time and a belief in the value of the experiential process.

TEACH CHILDREN TO REPLACE ANGER AND FEAR WITH PERSEVERANCE, INDERSTANDING AND COURAGE

There is a section in B.F. Skinner's *Walden Two* in which a visitor to the community is told how children are taught to deal with frustration by tying a lollipop around their necks. The children can eat the lollipop anytime they wish, but if they wait until the end of the day they can have all the lollipops they want. Skinner used this story to illustrate how important the ability to delay gratification is and how a rational community would aid in the development of this ability among its children. Perhaps we should be sending every child off to school each morning with a lollipop around their neck.

If a child can not conquer frustration, or regularly indulges his angry impulses, or is regularly fearful, the child will always be at the mercy of and remain dependent on others.

To illustrate this in my own family and others I have devised a simple technique. When a child continually allows the antics or behavior of a sibling to anger or frustrate them I make the first child the second child's slave for a brief period. Often, only a few minutes of this is enough for the first child to see how much power they are *giving* to their sibling and how little effort it actually takes to control themselves.

In my next book I plan to focus on strategies for developing perseverance, courage and understanding. At this point suffice it to say that without these characteristics no one truly becomes an adult. Furthermore these characteristics are incorporated into a person through *doing*.

WHEN IN DOUBT NEVER DO ANYTHING FOR A CHILD THAT THEY CAN OR SHOULD DO FOR THEMSELVES

Most parents can tie a child's shoe faster than the child can. Therefore, parents rarely need to practice shoe-tying.

Children need to practice more than adults.

Whenever possible let the child tie its own shoe. For a parent to do otherwise would give the child the covert message,

"You are stupid and helpless and I must take care of you."

After thirty years or so of these kind of messages you will be lucky if the child does not chop you into little pieces and stuff you down the garbage disposal.

A patient once told me,

"Doc, *you can lead a horse to water, but a goat will eat anything.*"

I chose to interpret this as a profound statement and not authentic Carolina redneck gibberish. I think what my eloquent patient meant was that there are different types of children though we treat them all the same. Some children are like horses that we can lead to water by providing opportunities to grow and learn. Other children, with different learning styles, are like the proverbial goat, which can survive off of the refuse of others. These children (the goats) need us just not to impede their growth and to get out of their way. Wise parents seem to know if their children are horses or goats and respond to them accordingly. All parents should encourage their children to do for themselves.

If you do not want your child to be a Fat Dog, do not keep them in the role of a child.

If this book was useful give it to a friend[*]**, if not feed it to your goat.**

---

[*] Actually, my publisher suggested it would be better if you bought ten copies and sent them to friends who are not as competent at parenting as you are.

APPENDIXES

These pages were meant to be torn from the book and displayed in a prominent location to remind you of the teachings from

FAT DOG DON'T RUN NO RABBIT

… we rejoice in our sufferings
knowing that our suffering produces endurance
and endurance produces character
and character produces hope
and hope does not disappoint us.

(Romans V: 3-5)

APPENDIX A

<u>FORTY-ONE REFLECTIONS FROM AFIELD</u>

1. THE TRUE MARK OF A FAT DOG IS THE DIFFICULTY THEY HAVE LEAVING HOME AND BECOMING AN ADULT.

2. REGARDLESS OF POOR PARENTING, BAD GENES, PEER PRESSURE, CHILDHOOD TRAUMA, STUPID CHOICES, SOCIAL INEQUITY OR EVEN ACTS OF GOD, BEING AN ADULT MEANS ACCEPTING RESPONSIBILITY FOR YOUR OWN BEHAVIOR, MAKING YOUR OWN LIFE AND CONTRIBUTING TO THE GREATER GOOD.

3. AN INDIVIDUAL MIGHT BE CONSIDERED OVERPRIVILEGED WHEN THE LINKS BETWEEN RIGHTS AND RESPONSIBILITIES HAVE BEEN CHRONCALLY AND

CONTIUOUSLY EVADED, ERODED OR IGNORED.

4. THE PRIMARY GOAL OF PARENTING IS TO HELP THE CHILD BECOME AN INDEPENDENT AND RESPONSIBLE ADULT. ACTIONS THAT CONTRIBUTE TO THIS GOAL ARE APPROPRIATE (PARENTING BEHAVIOR), WHILE ACTIONS THAT IMPEDE THIS GOAL ARE INAPPROPRIATE (PARENTING BEHAVIOR).

5. THE TRUE VALUE OF FREE WILL IS THAT IT PROVIDES A PROCESS FOR THE DEVELOPMENT OF VALUE.

6. RESPONSIBILITY LOGICALLY FLOWS FROM CHOICE. IF A CHILD IS NOT FREE TO CHOOSE, THEN THEY ARE LESS LIKELY TO ACCEPT PERSONAL RESPONSIBILITY AND TO BLAME OTHERS. BUT, IF A CHILD IS FREE TO CHOOSE WITHOUT

CONSEQUENCES THEY BECOME LESS RESPONSIBLE AND MORE DEPENDENT.

7. SUCCESSFULLY DEALING WITH FRUSTRATION IS ESSENTIAL IN THE ENJOYMENT OF LIFE, THE DEVELOPMENT OF OPTIMISM, THE ACCOMPLISHMENT OF INDEPENDENCE AND THE ATTAINMENT OF PERSONAL HAPPINESS.

8. ANYTHING WORTH DOING IS WORTH DOING POORLY.

9. FAT DOGS ARE PHOBIC OF FAILURE HAVING BEEN TRAINED TO BE SO BY WELL-MEANING PARENTS WHO DO NOT UNDERSTAND THE PROCESS OF FAILURE, JUST THE STATE OF FAILURE.

10. THE FAT DOG MAY NATURALLY POSSESS CERTAIN INADEQUACIES, BUT THE ACTIONS OF THE OVER-INDULGENT FAMILY

MAGNIFY, RITUALISE AND IN SOME CASES GLORIFY THESE SHORT-COMMINGS.

11. THE TIMES THAT THE MARTYR CHOOSES NOT TO SPEAK, OR BITES THEIR TONGUE, OR SUGAR COATS REALITY, THESE ARE THE TIMES THAT THE MARTYR PASSIVELY OBSTRUCTS THE PASSAGE OF THEIR CHILDREN FROM EGOCENTRIC PUPPIES TO WORTHWHILE ADULTS.

12. THE REAL MOTIVATION TO THE BEHAVIOR OF THE MARTYR IS PERSONAL FEAR OR THE AVOIDANCE OF PERSONAL PAIN.

13. THE MARTYR NEEDS THE FAT DOG SO MUCH IT IS IMPOSSIBLE FOR THEM TO BELIEVE THAT THE FAT DOG DOES NOT NEED THEM AS MUCH.

14. THE DIFFERENCE BETWEEN THE MARTYR'S REACTION AND THE REACTION OF A

HEALTHY PARENT IS THAT WHILE THE HEALTHY PARENT MIGHT HAVE THE SAME FEARS AS THE MARTYR THE HEALTHY PARENT DOES NOT ALLOW THESE FEARS TO INTERFERE WITH RESPONSIBLE AND RESPECTFUL ACTIONS.

15. FRUSTRATION, SACRIFICE, PRESSURE AND INTROSPECTION FORM THE CRUCIBLE FROM WHICH SELF-ESTEEM EMERGES.

16. IT IS IMPORTANT TO NOTE THAT CHILDREN DEVELOP SELF-ESTEEM WITH OUR SUPPORT AND GUIDANCE, BUT IF THEY ARE LACKING IN SELF-ESTEEM THEY MAY REQUIRE MORE ADVERSITY AND DISCIPLINE, NOT LESS.

17. UPON EXAMINATION THE "GOOD REASON" IS RAELY GOOD AND OFTEN LACKS REASON, WHEN IT IS USED TO JUSTIFY TREATING SOME ONE AS SPECIAL. THE "GOOD REASON" IS JUST AN EXCUSE. THE "GOOD

REASON" IS IRRESPONSIBLE AND BREEDS DEPENDENCY.

18. THE FEAR THAT THEY (FAT DOGS) MIGHT FAIL IS SO GREAT WITHIN THEM THAT THEY WASTE THEIR LIFE BEING WHAT THEY ARE RATHER THAN BECOMING WHAT THEY MIGHT BE.

19. BECAUSE THE MOTIVES OF THE FAT DOG ARE ALWAYS SELFISH, THEY BELIEVE THE MOTIVES OF OTHERS ARE SELFISH. THE FAT DOG BELIEVES EVERYONE FEELS AS WORTHLESS AND VALULESS AS THEY DO.

20. FAT DOGS HAVE DIFFICULTY PERCIEVING PLAY AS AN EXPERIENCE OF PLEASURABLE TRANSCEDENT LEARNING AND CONTINUALLY CORRUPT IT INTO AN OPPORTUNITY FOR EGO MAGNIFICATION.

21. TO PLAY IS TO LEARN WITHOUT FEAR.

22. **THERE MAY NOT BE A MORE EFFICIENT WAY TO MAKE SOME ONE HATE YOU THAN TO CONTINUALLY TREAT THEM AS THOUGH THEY ARE STUPID, WORTHLESS INADEQUATE AND HELPLESS.**

23. **THE DEPENDENCY OF THE FAT DOG IS INVERSELY RELATED TO THE INTIMACY BETWEEN THE PARENTS, OR THE DEPENDENCY OF THE FAT DOG INCREASES AS THE CONNECTIVENESS BETWEEN THE PARENTS DECREASES.**

24. **FOR FAT DOGS PUPPYHOOD IS DESIRABLE TO DOGHOOD BECAUSE PUPPIES DON'T HAVE TO CARE ABOUT ANYTHING OR ANYONE ELSE.**

25. **POWER AND WEALTH ARE NOT INTRINSICLY EVIL, BUT WE MUST REMEMBER THAT EVEN THOUGH THEY ARE**

NOT ALWAYS EARNED, THEY ALWAYS HAVE
A COST.

26. HOW MANY TIMES DO PARENTS AID IN THE
DESTRUCTION OF THEIR CHILDREN BY
TRYING TO GIVE THEM WHAT MUST BE
EARNED.

27. THE PRIMARY RELATIONSHIP IN A FAMILY
IS BETWEEN THE SPOUSES.

28. ADULTS FORM UNITS IN ALL CULTURES NOT
JUST TO PROMOTE THE SURVIVAL OF THE
SPECIES, BUT TO ALLOW FOR OPTIMAL
PERSONAL GROWTH.

29. ONE TELLTALE SIGN THAT THE MARITAL
RELATIONSHIP IS IMPROVING, IS THAT THE
FAT DOG IS NO LONGER THE CENTER OF
FAMILY CONCERN.

30. PARENTS SHOULD EXAMINE WHAT EXPERIENCES HELPED THEM DEVELOP INTO ADULTS AND SEEK TO PROVIDE SIMILAR OPPORTUNITIES FOR THEIR CHILDREN.

31. CHILDREN BECOME ADULTS BY DEVELOPING THE COURAGE TO FACE THEIR FEARS. PARENTS ARE NOT TRULY ADULTS UNTIL THEY FACE THEIR FEARS ABOUT THEIR CHILDREN.

32. REMEMBER,THE MOTHER DOG IS NOT DETERRED IN HER DUTY BY BEING CALLED A BITCH.

33. REMEMBER, CUTTING THE PUPPY OFF FROM YOUR DEPENDENCY IS ACTUALLY A VOTE OF CONFIDENCE.

34. EVEN THOUGH HUMANS START LIFE AS SELF-CENTERED, HELPLESS AND

DEPENDENT, MOST PEOPLE FIND THAT THEIR PERSONAL SURVIVAL IS BEST SERVED BY NOT JUST CARING FOR THEMSELVES, BUT CARING FOR OTHERS TOO.

35. IF YOU DO NOT THINK YOU CAN LOVE CHILDREN ENOUGH TO BE A GOOD PARENT, DON'T HAVE CHILDREN.

36. IF YOUR CHILD HAS TO STRUGGLE, RISK, SUFFER AND SOMETIMES BE UNHAPPY, THEN PERHAPS THEY CAN BECOME ADULTS AND NOT FAT DOGS.

37. IF A CHILD IS TOO FEARFUL OF FAILURE THEY ARE UNLIKELY TO RISK LEARNING NEW OR DIFFICULT SKILLS. IF A PARENT IS TOO FEARFUL OF THEIR CHILD'S FAILURE THEY WILL CONTINUALLY INTERVENE AND THE CHILD WILL NEVER KNOW WHETHER OR NOT THEY CAN SUCCEED ON THEIR OWN.

38. **WE MUST EXPECT OUR CHILDREN TO BECOME INDEPENDENT AND RESPONSIBLE ADULTS IF THEY ARE TO BELIEVE THAT THEY CAN, BUT WE MUST ACCEPT THAT THERE MAY BE SMALL FAILURES ALONG THE WAY.**

39. **IF A CHILD CAN NOT CONQUER FRUSTRATION, OR OFTEN INDULGES ANGRY IMPULSES, OR IS REGULARLY FEARFUL, THE CHILD WILL ALWAYS BE AT THE MERCY OF AND REMAIN DEPENDENT ON OTHERS.**

40. **CHILDREN NEED TO PRACTICE MORE THAN ADULTS.**

41. **IF YOU DO NOT WANT YOUR CHILD TO BECOME A FAT DOG DO NOT KEEP THEM IN THE ROLE OF A CHILD.**

APPENDIX B

<u>YOU MIGHT HAVE A FAT DOG IF ...</u>

- Your child continually demonstrates a lack of courage
- Your child gives up easily
- Your child would rather cling to you than play with peers
- Your child is not liked by most children
- Your child's allowance is more than you save monthly
- Your child refuses to eat anything except "special" foods

OR

- You believe your child's happiness is your responsibility
- You believe that your child can't make it in the real world
- You had rather tie your child's shoe than watch them struggle
- You choose to spend more time with your child than your spouse
- You have not taken a vacation in twenty-five years because you do not want to leave your child alone
- You still layout your child's clothes after the child is older than six

- You blame your child's friends for those six D.U.I. arrests
- You worry that your child will suffer from "empty nest syndrome" when you and your spouse are dead

OR

- Your thirty year old lives at home, has no job, dresses better than you, only needs three more semesters to graduate and has a great tan

If you can answer yes to two of the above items you might have a **Fat Dog.** If you can answer yes to three or more of the above statements you may need much more help than the **Fat Dog. Fat Dogs** are not born, they are trained and become the way they are through a process of chronic overprivilege.

APPENDIX C

<u>HOW TO MAKE A FAT DOG RUN</u>

STEP ONE: IMPROVE YOUR MARITAL RELATIONSHIP

STEP TWO: ESTABLISH SOUND PARENTING GOALS

STEP THREE: REMEMBER WHAT WORKED FOR YOU

STEP FOUR: LET GO OF THE BICYCLE

STEP FIVE: STARVE THE PUPPY

These steps are to be taken in the order they are presented and should build on each other. As parents move through these steps there should be discernible movement on the part of the **Fat Dog.** As they say in 12-step groups, "half measures avail us nothing," so the steps must be consistent and continuous. The **Fat Dog** must be convinced that the parents really mean business, and that life as they knew it is changing. Only in extreme cases should parents have to proceed to the sixth step, but when they take the first step they should be prepared to take the final step.

APPENDIX D

<u>CHARACTERISTICS COMMONLY ASSOCIATED WITH HEALTHY MARITAL RELATIONSHIPS</u>

- **INDIVIDUAL GROWTH IS ENCOURAGED AND REWARDED**

- **THE SPOUSES ARE INTERDEPENDENT AND NOT CO-DEPENDENT**

- **DECISION-MAKING FOR THE MOST PART IS COLLABORATIVE**

- **THE COUPLE HAS REGULAR TIME TOGETHER AND OCASSIONALLY EXCLUSIVELY COUPLE TIME APART FROM THE FAMILY**

- **MARITAL RELATIONSHIP ISSUES ARE NOT WORKED OUR THROUGH THE CHILDREN**

- **EACH SPOUSE BELIEVES THE OTHER WOULD ALWAYS INTEND HIM OR HER WELL, NOT ILL**

- **ALL THINGS BEING EQUAL, WHEN GIVEN A CHOICE, SPOUSES CHOOSE THE COMPANY OF EACH OTHER**

- **COMMUNICATION BETWEEN SPOUSES IS RESPECTFUL, HONEST AND DIRECT**

APPENDIX E

<u>THE FIVE GOALS OF PARENTING</u>

THE FIRST GOAL OF PARENTING IS TO HELP CHILDREN BECOME INDEPENDENT AND RESPONSIBLE ADULTS

THE SECOND GOAL OF PARENTING IS TO HELP CHILDREN BECOME ALTRUISTIC AND COMPASSIONATE

THE THIRD GOAL OF PARENTING IS TO HELP CHILDREN DEVELOP RATIONAL THINKING SKILLS

THE FOURTH GOAL OF PARENTING IS THE TRANS-GENERATIONAL INCULCATION OF VALUES

THE FIFTH GOAL OF PARENTING IS TO HELP THE SPECIES NOT JUST SURVIVE BUT TO FLOURISH

APPENDIX F

THE LESSON

If you live your life through them
If you have cared and cared and cared
If you meet their every whim

If you tears seem never dry
If you always wonder why

If you are sorry they you sired
If you fear a living death

If your legs and lungs are tired
If you have just one more breath

LET GO OF THE BICYCLE!!!

(FLQ 9/6/03)

APPENDIX G

<u>LOVING YOUR CHILD</u>

LOVING YOUR CHILD MEANS STANDING WITH YOUR CHILD IN THE DARKNESS OF THEIR FEARS SO THAT THEY CAN LEARN THE COURAGE TO CONFRONT FEAR

LOVING YOUR CHILD MEANS ACTIVELY ATTEMPTING TO GIVE YOUR CHILD WHAT THEY NEED. MOST OFTEN WHAT THEY NEED IS TO BE LOVED.

LOVING YOUR CHILD MEANS ACCEPTING THE IMPERFECTIONS AND FAILURE REQUIRED TO BECOME A HEALTHY ADULT

LOVING YOUR CHILD MEANS TEACHING YOUR CHILD HOW TO FLOURISH

LOVING YOUR CHILD MEANS LETTING THEM GO SO THEY CAN FIND <u>THEIR</u> WAY HOME

LOVING YOUR CHILD MEANS LOVING THEM FOR WHO THEY ARE

ABOUT THE AUTHOR

Dr. Frank L. Quinn is a therapist, educator and researcher with over twenty-five years of clinical experience. He is currently a partner in Carolina Psychiatric Services, P. A., where he serves as Clinical Director of Outpatient Services. Additionally, he is the founder and Director of the South Carolina Center for Gambling Studies, and serves as an adjunct professor of psychology at Columbia College. Although well known throughout the southeast for his lectures on families and addiction, his research on electronic gambling (especially video poker) is familiar with audiences throughout the United States, Canada and Australia.

A graduate of the University of North Carolina, Chapel Hill (AB & MS) and the University of South Carolina (Ph.D.), Dr. Quinn currently resides in Columbia, S.C. with his wife Lane and their three children.

Printed in the United States
18114LVS00005B/292